Buttermilk Book Publishing

Myrtle Beach, South Carolina

Copyright T. Allen Winn 2020

All Rights Reserved

This book is a biography of Clay Page based on interviews and the singer-songwriter's actual accounts of a life devoted to music.

Typecast in Times New Roman

ISBN 978-1-7331576-7-4

Clay Page

Somewhere In Between

Dedication

My biography is dedicated to my family, friends, my fans, and anyone I might have done wrong along the way, or those that might have treated me wrongly. It is all about forgiveness and faith in God, following His plan and believing in Him. Life is too short. Look for the good in it and learn to love the journey.

For merchandise and show dates www.claypagecountry.com
claypagebookings@gmail.com
Follow @claypagemusic
For downloads go to Spotify, Apple Music and most streaming platforms

A Clay 'Page' Turner by the Chapters

You Can't Pretty Up Pondering
Same Sad Song
Pure Country
School Daze
Southbound
From Idol to Full Throttle
Digging in the Dirt
Something
Same Old Song, New Beginnings
Mother Knows Best
The Miracle Child
Making a Difference When a Difference Counts
Mister Fix It
Let It Shine
Somewhere Down the Road
Southern Fried Morning Show
Historical Ramifications
From the Author T. Allen Winn

You Can't Pretty Up Pondering

Clay Page prepares for a road trip, one that will take him from his home in Elberton, Georgia through South Carolina, ending in Charlotte, North Carolina. It is November 6, 2019. He has a few things yet to tidy up before leaving his humble surroundings in the Peach State. Clay is at a pertinent crossroad in his young twenty-five-year-old life. Serious decisions are dogging him. His life in general is filled with a slew of challenges yet a truck load of optimism. Undaunted, he presses onward knowing things happen for a reason, and if you are patient all things work out sooner or later, and hopefully for the best. He is more than ten years into this investment. Ten years might not sound like a long time, but it represents over half of young Clay's life thus far. This is significant on any scale. First things first. Clay finishes helping his grandfather James and then he will set out on today's journey.

Sometimes solitude can be your friend. Other times it can be a mortal enemy. Having time to reflect and think through situations can help one gain clarity on the challenges that are mounting, or it might just muddy up the already trouble waters. Too much thinking and not enough solving the problems at hand. Clay will be flying solo on this trip. His hands will be on the wheel, eyes on the road, and a mind racing with solutions to unanswered questions. Loading up his vehicle, Clay switches on the ignition, shifts into drive, and motors down the driveway. Let the pondering begin as only Clay can ponder. A three-hour drive will allow ample time to reflect and reminiscence. His journey begins at home for now. As he prepares to leave Clay reflects.

> "You must do what needs to be done when it comes to supporting family before taking care of the personal business at hand. Keeping things in perspective I am just finishing up working on a storage building with my granddaddy James. Man, we have been working on this building for three days. I told Papa James I could help him with it until noon, but then I needed to be on the road and headed to Charlotte. Before leaving though, I better check the oil and the fluids in my vehicle. She has been known to run hot on occasion. It has been a good one otherwise and takes me where I need to go, or at least it has up until now.

A car with 300, 000 miles on it cannot be expected to live forever. It is probably already on borrowed time but it's all I have. Babying it is about all I can do. I can only hope that it gets me to Charlotte and back home. She is an old hand-me-down Isuzu Rodeo that my Papa Ricky bought for me in 2012. The car and I have shared some memories. We have traveled our fair share of places as well.

Clay with his Legendary Rodeo

It seems I am surrounded by symbolic reminders of my humble lifestyle. Living in a 480-square foot square cabin located on my Uncle Norman's land has a way of grounding me and keeping my life in perspective. I always say never forget your roots. I inherited this land from my dearly departed Uncle Norman. It is where I call home as I pursue my dream of becoming an established musical artist. The task ahead after finishing helping my granddaddy is to load up the old rambling wreck and head toward Charlotte. My mind is spinning. My head is filled with more things than my brain can keep up with, so it feels.

I am certainly in a weird spot in my career right now. Looming large is my struggle with seeking the perfect match for management. I have offers on the table and I have been doing my best to dissect some of the management contracts that have been presented. Over the past few days my buddy Troy Curtis in Nashville has been helping me understand these and focus on key points. There is no denying it, I know I need help with my career, but I am apprehensive about making any knee jerk or dumb decisions where it is concerned.

Compounding everything, financially it is extremely tight right now. I am at this spot where I don't feel I need to play somewhere every week in this local market, and I have been playing nonstop for the past ten years. I am kind of over the urge to play in smoky bars or being background music every weekend just to make a few bucks. I am in a vicious personal struggle with this because I do have bills to pay. These gigs do supplement my income. I just have larger aspirations and this life complicates my career visions. This car I am driving damn sure isn't getting any better either. See what I mean. I have too much going on in this crazy head of mine.

What little bit I have built to this point has been on my own. I am the epitome of the self-made man if ever there was one. I am not bragging nor feeling sorry for myself. It is what it is. Therefore, I find myself in such a vicious struggle right now. Just the mere thought of handing this away and giving someone else the steering wheel in my life is tough for me to comprehend. I must be confident that having a manager is the right thing for me and it is the sensible choice to carry me to that next step.

Honestly, I cannot really say I have done everything on my own because I have had plenty of good people helping me along the way. There have been great inspirational mentors in my journey thus far. I am not on a record label nor do I have a management contract. That is just a fact. I am ready, though, to do something if I can figure out what that something might be.

Boy, I find myself in a self-therapy session, soul searching, and having time to think as I ride in my old relic. I wasn't exactly prepared to be going down this road today. It must be something I need. There is something that weighs even heavier on my mind this month. It is a bit stressful if I must be honest with myself. It has to do with my albums. Everyone that I have completed required me taking out a loan from a bank to pay for the investment in my career…on my shoulders all the way. People that are not in this business have no idea what it cost to cut an album. The bank knows me well. It is already November 6, and I've got my next one scheduled for release November 22. Bless her heart, my grandmother Camilla insisted that she give me a helpful loan to do this one. She told me she did not want me paying interest to the bank. She would not take no for an answer. I love my grandma dearly.

One thing leads to another. I cannot help but think about the marketing aspect of this release. Am I doing all the things, all the right things, that I can do to make this successful? Generating income is the name of the game so that I can quickly repay my grandmother. I want to make her proud of me, but she insists she is not worried about it. She tells me she is already proud of me. She says she does not want me to pay it back if I don't have it. My pride says something different though. Paying her back is a priority. This just takes me in circles wondering if I am moving in the right direction in my career. I am literally the one man show right now. I'm writing and recording the music, marketing the music, and booking the gigs. It is overwhelming at times. Here I am, still at that spot where I can spend all day on my business and neglect my creative side. This just leads to a stressful environment. I'm sure others have traveled this path as well.

I need to be creative. I need to handle the business. I need to repay my grandmother. I need to focus on this trip to Charlotte. What I really need is a few more of me. I have committed to doing the AMG (Artist Music Guild) Heritage Awards in Charlotte to acknowledge all forms of artistry. They reached out to me after I was on American

Idol. From what I know about them they are nonprofit and donate instruments to schools for kids with parents who are unable to pay for them. It just felt like a worthy way to give back. Other American Idol contestants will be there as well as a few headliner artists. Part of the three-day event will be our mentoring some of these kids.

This is for a worthy cause, but the timing is not good for me. This is strictly a volunteer event. We receive no compensation for appearing. I am footing the cost for the drive plus hotel and food expenses. For three days I will be committed and donating my time as they request, but it is going to tap me big time. If you do good things, then sometimes good things happen as a result. I have no regrets about doing it other than it is just tough on me right now expense wise. I never want anyone to see me as this uncaring giant asshole. I do care and I do want to give back anyway that I can. My life is just in a complicated stage right now. I am at a crossroad. It tends to build character I suppose. I must learn to practice patience. That is easier said than done.

Crazy thoughts can sure boggle my brain though. Family is important to me. I have been thinking about my little brother Connor. He started driving for the first time two weeks ago. It is funny, me thinking about him growing up and my sister being in college at the University of Georgia. She has had a tough time adjusting to college and being away from home. The college experience doesn't always agree with everyone. I really look up to my sister, even though she is my little sister. She is as pure as they come. She has always had a good head on her shoulders. I always worry about those two, hoping they are all right. My girlfriend Maggie Jameson is on her way to Myrtle Beach right now. I was hoping she could make the trip with me. I'm sure she wishes I could have been going with her as well. We have been together for eight years. She is one of the good ones.

My brain is running the gambit. Of all things, my mom and I had a little misunderstanding recently. She lives across the road from me. I catch myself eyeing my phone waiting for her to call me. No doubt in my mind she is going to call me while I am driving to Charlotte to find out where I am, or for me to let her know when I arrive. I can hear her now, 'Don't be on the phone. Buckle up.' We are so much alike, and we tend to key in on similar things.

Sometimes you just have no choice as to where the memories take you. This is one of those times for better or worse. Mama and Daddy did not really get along, divorcing when I was in middle school. I had a conversation with my dad a few weeks ago, possibly the most grownup conversation we have ever had. I struggled to honor him the way that I probably should, but I was just a kid then. What did I really know about honoring anyone? I was too young to fully understand the circumstances in their marriage and lives. It was easier for me to disrespect him after witnessing the verbal conflicts going on between them. I tended to take mama's side, being caught in the middle. Now older, I can see how my mom was right sometimes and my dad right other times, and how each could be equally wrong. Life lesson. I can see the same in myself. There were times where I was sometimes right but often wrong as well in my thinking and interpretation of the situations. I am glad I had this conversation with both recently, explaining to them how I could have done a better job honoring them both, telling them I forgave them for their actions in these matters. Guess it is never too late.

I am ready to move forward and leave the past in the past. I am no longer interested in the rhetoric of who has done this and who hasn't. Mama and Daddy, I love you both. Thanks for everything you have done and continue to do. Time to clear the slate, a new beginning because life is too short to be focused on all the negatives.

I relayed to them how I watched Uncle Norman pass and was the only one there when he died. Watching somebody that you love die changes your whole perspective on life. This has put me on the path of something new, an entirely different outlook on life. It's funny how a simple drive can make a person reassess one's worth on this earth, the good, bad and the ugly of it. It can be a cleansing experience. I have a long drive; no telling where this will end up taking me.

Well here I am, in South Carolina passing through Calhoun Falls. I have fond memories of coming over here from Elberton as a kid to visit my grandma, Nanny Carolyn. I spent plenty of times here with her and my two cousins. My grandma was tasked with watching my cousins. I would see them when I came to her house. My cousins Ricky and Drake Smith are brothers. Boy did we have some wild and crazy times growing up together. We could do some stupid stuff. It is shameful to think on it now, but we used to pick on this one kid something terrible. I have no explanation as to why except that we were mean. There is a chance I was probably the meanest in the group. Which is not something I am proud of now. I feel bad just thinking about we treated this boy. We surely deserved having our butts torn up for the things we did to him. I learned what bullying really was when I was in high school and on the receiving end of it. What goes around indeed comes around.

We sure were mean to this kid my grandma kept. All because he owned this little white and pink or purple looking bicycle. We didn't think his bike was cool for a boy. Now I owe him my most humble apology for the way I treated him. I really should look him up and make this legit. I now realize just how serious and damaging picking on him and the impact it can forever have on a person. It is not anything to be taken lightly. I am ashamed of the kid I was back then. Being a little kid certainly does not give me a free pass. I own what I did and am sorry for it.

It must have been something in the air when I visited Calhoun Falls that brought the worst out in me. It was an evil adrenalin rush. Ricky and Drake had their moments as well, often picking fights with one another. Rough and tumble seemed to be the recipe for our outdoor antics. Kids being kids is not always pretty though. An afternoon might be filled with its fair share of feuding and fighting with each other but at the end of day, we would forgive and forget, and be friends again. We would then be back out there riding our Big Wheels. The joy in our life was spending afternoons riding Big Wheels and bicycles at her house. Everybody had a Big Wheel then. We were quite serious about racing them. It was nothing for someone to get mad, accusing someone else of cheating on the Big Wheel during our staged races. I can only imagine some of the dirt that those two might tell on me now."

A big wheel is a brand of low-riding tricycles made mostly of plastic with a larger front wheel. Introduced by Louis Marx and Company in 1969 and manufactured in Girard, Pennsylvania, the big wheel was a very popular toy in the 1970s in the United States. This was partly because of its low cost and partly because consumer groups said it was a safer alternative to the traditional tricycle or bicycle. It was marketed primarily to boys between eight and ten years of age, and thus significantly bigger and older users than traditional tricycles.

The Big Wheel's popularity outlived the company that first introduced it. When Marx went out of business in 1985, Carolina Enterprises, known later as Enterprise Industries, produced the Big Wheel for a second generation of mobile American kids. Coleco offered a similar vehicle, as did Playskool, Gearbox Toys, General Foam Plastics, and Razor USA. Today, the Big Wheel has been revitalized by Alpha International, Inc. of Cedar Rapids, Iowa, to carry new generations of kids on sidewalk adventures.

"Time sure flies when my mind is racing almost as fast as I'm driving this old Rodeo. I am now skirting past Abbeville, South Carolina, and the hospital where I was born. Yep, that's where my sixteen-year-old mama birthed me."

Abbeville has plenty of history. It is called the birthplace and the deathbed of the Confederacy. Secession Street in Abbeville is where it all started. It is the location where they met in 1860 to make their plans to secede from the United States. They named it Session Hill and the street does go up a long hill. Confederate President Jefferson Davis stopped in Abbeville after fleeing from Richmond, Virginia when the Confederacy was supposedly on the brink. He stayed at the historical Burt-Stark Mansion and history says that that is where he officially called it quits for the Confederate government in 1865.

Clay remained immersed in his thoughts as he motored his Rodeo toward Charlotte, hoping the old car would complete the journey drama free. His car overheating, delaying, or preventing his arrival would not set well for those depending on him being there. Some of the American Idol alumni were supposed to be in the lineup along with a few headliners. He had already covered the gambit of memories, good and bad, many he had not been prepared to remember. That is the thing about nostalgia. It does not necessarily come at you in any desired order. Sometimes it seems to have a mind of its own. It was all good though. Most memories are, even those seemingly too painful to relive. Regrets are always a part of life. Life does not often offer opportunities to do things over and make the wrongs right. The past is the past. Right now, Clay tries to keep focused on the future, his future. Moments are triggered just the same. Rehashing life's incidences are just part of the plan, so it seems today. Nothing to do but go with the flow.

> "Wow! Where has the time gone? I am entering onto Interstate 85 in Greenville, S.C. I'd better pay close attention because folks tend to drive like maniacs on 85. Toss in tons of construction work and this could be a tough part of the route to Charlotte. Rodeo don't fail me now. I always think about my granddaddy, Papa Ricky, when I'm on 85. My grandma Camilla still lives nearby in Powdersville. I wish I had time to stop. I wonder what she is doing today. It seems to always go back to this. My grandma was at my mom's this week and that is when she decided to help me out financially. We were sitting around the dinner table at Mama's Sunday and she asked if she needed to throw me a few dollars to get me through the week. She wanted to help me out a little bit. I thanked her but told her that wasn't helping me. I explained how I did not want to be dependent on anyone. I hope I didn't hurt her feelings. She loves me. She just wanted to help.
>
> This just piles on to that weird spot I am in my career right now. There is a lot that people don't understand about this business and where my pride plays into it. I am fortunate to have done considerably well standing on my own two feet. I could pick up the phone right now and could call anyone of about a hundred venues. I could be booked and paying my bills, making a little extra money, and things would be great. That is not my goal right now though. Doing that would water down my brand at this point in my career. This works against me as I am attempting to emerge into that next phase of my career. I could easily play somewhere in Greenville tonight and be background music for the venue. It would financially do volumes to help me out on this trip, but if I do that, I will fall quickly back into that same realm that I have been in for the past ten years. I don't want to do this while I have momentum on my side. The key is for me to use this momentum to my advantage. If I don't, I could

easily slide back into the place I used to be. I have no desire to return to square one. It is all about the marketing and my dilemma at hand. Should I be going with a manager and contract or not?

Passing though here reminds me of how my granddaddy, Papa Ricky Haggarty, who bought me the Rodeo, could scare the crap out of me when behind the wheel driving down 85. Right before he became sick and passed, I would be riding with him and he would be paying little attention to everything around him. That is not something you should do on 85. I can see him now swerving over into the other lanes, whistling, or talking, not a care in the world. I can vividly hear that whistling, something he did all the time. I would be sitting beside him about to flip out thinking we were going to hit these folks in cars around us.

Before he got diagnosed with cancer, he called me to ask for help on some of the odd jobs he was doing. After working in construction for years he was not the type to sit around and do nothing. He did about everything from mowing lawns to pressure washing for people. He also worked with a Christmas Tree farm in Powdersville. He could work circles around me. I remember helping him with a pressure wash job. There he was dealing with cancer, me being a young twenty-three-year-old, and he was still more of a man that I was. That generation possessed phenomenal work ethics. Those work ethics inspired me. I always worked hard. Working side by side with him put a new perspective on it for me. Looking back now I realize how much I cherished those times.

I am approaching Highway 385 exit from Greenville S.C. to Columbia S.C., remembering that Maggie called me before I left Elberton. She was in Columbia heading to Myrtle Beach, still a couple of hours remaining in her drive. I see exit 51A ahead. This just triggers more thoughts. My buddy Jimmy Jones, whom I grew up with in Elberton, lives right here in Simpsonville. I am super excited for what Jimmy is doing with his life. He is out of the Marines and working at the Greenville-Spartanburg

International Airport. I'm envious of his job because I just had my first opportunity to fly commercially last year. It came about because of a vacation posed after my Papa Ricky Haggerty died. My grandma Camilla and Papa Ricky always wanted to take the family on a cruise. It never fell into place for whatever reason. My grandparents were not rich by any stretch, but they made a decent living. They have always made sure that nobody else goes without though. Others come before them. They have forever been givers. They will go without to make sure others do not. After his death she told us how they had always wanted to take us on a cruise. She would have it no other way than to fulfill that dream in his memory. We flew out of Atlanta to the cruise destination.

That takes me back to thinking about Jimmy and him being an aircraft mechanic. Since flying I have gained a fascination with flying. My grandmama's home was right across from the little rural airport. I guess even as a little kid I was fascinated with watching the planes take off and land. This guy Chunk Patterson took me on my very first plane ride at that airport.

We went up in Chunk's plane when I was too young to really appreciate the experience. I was afraid and did not really want to do it. Chunk started out by just riding me in the cockpit down the airstrip. He then asked me, 'Are you sure you don't want to fly?' I must have given in. I can only vaguely remember going up though.

After the commercial flight experience, my fascination with flying has blossomed. Hindsight, if music weren't so important to me now, maybe I would consider something in the field of aviation. Then again, the mix of musicians and airplanes has not been the best combination. Think about it. There have been too many crashes ending too many careers. I am envious of Jimmy and what appears to be a great job for him while I follow my path in the music industry. He is doing well for himself. I am super proud for him. My pal Jimmy could tell some tales about us, just how mean we really were back in the day.

Jimmy and I grew up in a time where most may have pegged us as being less fortunate. I never thought about it like that thinking I had everything I wanted. We were not with the high rollers, but we did all right. I guess we were middle class. Our parents worked hard to provide for us. They were blue collar. My mama worked doing a little bit of everything. Jimmy and I were cut from the same cloth. Our paths were similar, our families having their fair share of ups and downs. I have several close buddies, but he and I just seemed to click. I still think about Tyler McKellar, Derek Johnson, and Barron Busby, the four of us being the crew back in the day. We hung out at Lake Russel and Bobby Brown Park near Elberton. Derek Johnson was from Calhoun Falls. He was a couple of years older than the rest of us and was the only one driving at the time. He was our designated big brother. He would drive us to the park to cruise for chicks. We would boast about how we were going there to pick up girls. Truth be told, we never got out of the car when there. We were more talk than anything else. We did a lot of gawking but were harmless otherwise.

Jimmy and I recently had a conversation about how he was in a transition spot in his life. I am doing the same where my music is concerned. I am super blessed with what I have accomplished even though doubts and challenges remain. Jimmy told me that he didn't realize that it was going to be so hard, being grown and on our own. I can say one thing about him, he straight up works his butt off. He must clock in and clock out every workday. I caught myself comparing where I was in relation to his situation. I told him nobody understood what there was to this music stuff. Thinking back now, I feel I might have come across like I was trying to one up him saying my situation was tougher than his. I should not have taken that stance with him. I am blessed to do what I do. After I said it, I had that little guilt tug for saying it the way I did. It was so wrong of me comparing my life to what he is doing. I do owe Jimmy an apology. Knowing him he probably thought what a prick I was, me playing music for a living. I am surprised he didn't call me out over it.

Maybe at age 25 the light finally comes on in your head and you begin seeing things differently. I for one am going through a phase, an obvious turning point, reassessing my situation. I feel Jimmy is struggling with it as well. Jimmy and I have always played music together. Jimmy's dad, David, played an instrumental role in me following the music path and playing in a band. David Jones had the Broad River Band. I guess I envied that life back then.

Jimmy and I used to skateboard at my mom's house. We were what I called redneck or hillbilly skateboarders. We would watch skateboard videos and then watch Hank Williams Jr. videos. After skateboarding we would venture inside to my bedroom and try to learn a Hank William's Jr. songs on our guitars. This was long before we were old enough to drive. Oddly, we began to click, a duo, the beginning of a band.

David Jones would take us Wednesday nights to open mic night in Elberton at Whitney's café off the Elberton Square. We would usually do a couple of songs. Mama would sometimes take us to Charly T's at the lake in Anderson, S.C. for open mic there. We thought we were cool. We would come into school the next day telling our buddies how tired we were after doing a show the night before, even though we were only there about an hour and were home by eight o'clock. We were celebrities in our own minds and that was our roadshow reality.

Clay and Jimmy Picking

Jimmy and I traveled the open mic circuit for a while. After we began driving, we formed our first band in high school, the birth of the Clay Page Band. Imagine that. It is crazy rehashing this stuff now. We were driving and would play a show here and there. Oh man, even before we could drive, we would load my PA in the back of my mama's Tahoe, and she would drive us to our show. Mama bought me my first PA system at Stan's Music World in Elberton for fifteen hundred bucks. She bought it out of money she did not have. She was a single mom at that point. I probably took things for granted, not realizing how she struggled to make ends meet. I should have known though. Our home was foreclosed on while I was in high school. She did what she could to make sure we did not go without, but times were hard. At the end of the day my mom and dad were kids raising a kid. I honestly couldn't imagine raising a baby then. I'm still 'growing up.'

The Clay Page Band

A lot of my influence of music comes from my dad and my mama both. Papa James as well. My dad, Rodney, bought me my first guitar from Stan's Music World in Elberton. It was on special for $100. It was a New York Pro. I still have it. Looking back, which seems to be what I am doing a lot of today, I thought I knew it all. Truth be known, I didn't know anything. I started playing guitar when I was nine or ten taking lessons when I was ten or eleven.

It is funny how the memories return from just passing by Jimmy's exit. Anytime I think about him, I think about playing music. It was such a big part of our lives. I just wanted to play the guitar. I didn't have a desire to sing. Playing the guitar was good enough for me, something I just enjoyed doing. Jimmy and I would sit around playing and I might bust out a note or two, but they didn't get any further than in my bedroom. I used to go to Uncle Norman's who lived just across the road from where I grew up. We lived on a dead-end dirt road. The road was like a peninsula on the lake. Driving down it, there was water on both sides of the road. Most of my family lived on this stretch. I spent much of my time when I was around eight at my grandma's in Calhoun Falls.

From age 9 to 13 I spent my summers at home hanging out with Uncle Norman. He lived across from us. He had an old Harmony guitar and showed me a few cords on it. After spending time with me doing that I guess he saw some potential and said, 'We need to get you some guitar lessons.' Mama and Daddy were still together then. They agreed to the guitar lessons. Vernon Brown lived in Calhoun Falls. He charged less than $10 for 30 minutes of lessons. Vernon is one of the slickest guitar players I have ever heard. He and I still talk on the phone occasionally. While hanging out with Uncle Norman, I remember that Mama had a karaoke machine before I owned a sound system. While learning how to play guitar from Vernon, I would then come home and experiment with singing. It is something that just slipped up on me. Uncle Norman was my audience. I would not play and sing around anyone else then. I gravitated to Hank Williams' songs. I did it to impress Uncle Norman because he put so much time and interest into my music. He was my greatest influence and my only audience.

Uncle Norman has passed. and I now live on the place where he once had his single wide mobile home. Living there has been a spiritual experience for me. It was where it all started for me with him supporting me. While playing around with that karaoke machine, Uncle Norman came up with the idea that I needed to play at the Calhoun Falls Town Wide Yard Sale. The yard sale was a huge annual event for the town and still is. He would not take no for an answer. He told me he had talked to John David and told me, 'You and little Jimmy are going to Calhoun Falls and sing a song at the street dance.' I flat told him I was not going to do it. He wasn't buying it. He told me I needed to do it. Uncle Norman won out. I ended up giving into his notion. I can picture Jimmy Jones and me that night at the street dance on that stage. I was fourteen and I was so nervous that I had an MP3 Player in one ear listening to the song we were playing. A video was made of our performance and it can still be seen on YouTube. That earplug can be seen in my ear right before we started playing. Fourteen years old and we were playing Whiskey Bent and Hell Bound for a town wide yard sale event. I didn't even know what I was singing. I was just singing. It sounded absolutely terrible, but people loved it. That night lit the fire in me to start playing more. It was indeed a pivotal point for me, to have this desire to play live shows and become serious about music.

Fourteen, what a beginning. Then I rocked along with a few high school buddies in a group with Jimmy Jones playing guitar and bass, Mitch Coker playing lead guitar. Cody Strickland from Ware Shoals, S.C. was on drums. Jimmy and Mitch played in the band when we were sixteen or seventeen and then Cody joined us. This was the one and only Clay Page Band. They played with me until I was around nineteen. Boy, I had reached a point then that I was taking the music super seriously, but I did not think any of the others were. Unfortunately, this eventually led to parting ways. I hope there are no hard feelings because of what went down. I personally call them friends today and I love these boys. You learn something from each and every person God puts in your life regardless of circumstances. I was ready to take it to a new level and to improve takes practice.

I cannot help wondering that because I was introverted. It made people perceive me as cocky and egotistical, even the guys I loved playing music with. I guess it is or was a little 'all about Clay' but it was my name hanging on the band name. Cody actually signed up for Battle of the Bands and we didn't have a name, so he suggested that we call it The Clay Page Band. Jimmy and I are best friends, but I remember us almost getting into a fight when we were playing in Greenville. It was about to break into a sure enough fight about him not changing his bass strings. We were sixteen, maybe seventeen and we still laugh about that incident. I think Mitch might have been siding with Jimmy, and we were all pissed off for a bit. We crashed at my grandma's in Powdersville, and after a nap, everything was good. I guess that was our first taste of band drama. I felt we were building a brand. We have remained buddies.

Thinking back on the band drama, there were times when a band member did not show up or maybe didn't do their part. I interpreted that as nearly being the end of the world. Now I see it differently. The show must go on regardless of circumstances. Professionals in this industry do not allow hiccups to derail them. I was just too much of a perfectionist to allow any wiggle room. Something my daddy told me has always stuck in my head. He said, 'If you're not going to do it right, you may as well not do it at all.' I cannot help but go back to those work ethics I learned from my granddaddy and my daddy. Boy…is this helping me learn some things about myself or what? It is just in my genes that I expect things to be a certain level, a higher standard. I know how much I put into what I do, and I guess I expect everyone else involved to do the same. It doesn't always work out that way though.

In high school, the infancy of the Clay Page Band, I was proud of where we were. We were tight as a band. I am equally as proud of that ensemble of band members. We could hold our own against most bands. We were doing well, but then I hit a brick wall. For whatever reason it became less enjoyable for me. It was a fine line between being professional and too professional to a point it was no longer fun. I had reached the point where members missing a note here and there grated on me. It was that perfection thing that I am afflicted with. The group was super tight still, but the fun had long expired for me personally. I just about quit playing music for a spell. Truth is, I had this girlfriend that was weighing heavy on my thinking too. She did not attempt to influence me to not play and she enjoyed my music, but I thought that I was in love. Love tends to cloud your normal thinking. It will win out over everything else, or it did back then.

Dealing with the band and its drama were getting tough for me to cope with. I guess true love gave me an exit strategy. I was sixteen and I had a driver's license. There was just too much happening not to take time and enjoy it. You get one shot at this. You cannot go back and relive your youth once it is gone. Assessing it now, I guess I just needed that break. Being head over heels with someone fills the void for sure. In love, there is no greater feeling, especially for a teenager. Love, just plain and simple, had trumped my passion for music. This ended up being a six-month hiatus away from what I thought I wanted to do. Uncle Norman noticed that I had drifted away from music and it obviously concerned him. Even he could not talk sense into someone bitten by the lovebug.

Like many wonderful love stories, sometimes it does not end as you visualize or hope. She and I eventually hit that point and split up. Another shameful admission in this little trip through my past; I put a fist through a wall at my mama's house the very night it ended. From in love to having my heart broken at age sixteen is not an easy pill to swallow. My mama nor the rest of my immediate family seemed to be nearly as torn up about this as I was. It was obvious that they were not heartbroken, end of that story. I decided then that I would not allow another flame to come between me and my music. I swore to it and still live by that mantra. I never said I wouldn't fall for another girl though. There is no need to swear to stuff that you know won't happen.

After a short break I reclaimed the Clay Page Band once again. This time I dropped the band part from the actual name. I revived it as just Clay Page. I formed a backup group made up of some old and some new musicians. I put more focus and emphasis on the fact that it was my name out there if we stunk or did well. I expected anyone who played with me to honor this as well. My new mindset was to keep the friendships out of it and treat it as a profession with higher standards inferred. I was now running a business, not something to just have fun with, party, and drink at the venues.

Girls...funny how they have this way of working back into the scene. I was a senior in high school and found myself in another relationship. I approached this one differently, lesson learned. I liked where she and I were. I felt her folks were okay with me as well and that was saying a lot. I was a punk back then with earrings in both ears. It wasn't just my earrings but attitude too. I am older now and would probably kick a daughter's butt for dating somebody like me. That was my rebel and renegade stage. Musicians had certain outrageous images to portray and I lived for that. I was playing the early Brantley Gilbert southern rock music and looking the part was important. This girl was a sweet girl. I cannot believe I'm going back there. The relationship was not perfect, and it was far from my true love experience. She had a younger sister that was dating a guy. I wasn't too crazy about that grated on me. I was a bit pissed or even jealous that at a younger age they felt they had the same privileges as we did. They had not earned that right, just starting to drive a car and all. I felt I had proved myself to her folks and they hadn't.

We were in Athens, Georgia and had to wait until the night closed out before the venue would fork over the pay. We were still teenagers. I didn't collect any pay that night because it was well past her curfew. We were with my mama that night. It was not like she had been hauled off to Athens unchaperoned. It hit me the wrong way, her folks not working with me in that situation. I forgive them today. Looking back now, they were probably just doing what most parents should do when your daughter is dating a punk liked I was then.

This takes me to another night in South Carolina when I was partying at my friend house, Cody Strickland's house. That is where I met Maggie. She and I have now been together eight years. We traveled similar paths back then. We have honestly learned from a lot of mistakes we have made along the way. She lost her dad, Donnie Jameson, to a car accident when she was only eight or nine years old. Life is not perfect, and we have our differences, but we work through them. We need each other to a degree. We've both had a tough row to hoe, but we learned from our hardships, and have paid for past mistakes. We are not perfect, and we will always make more mistakes in life. I try my best to blaze the right path and do the right things. I believe in asking God for direction when I am unsure about where I should go.

Funny...I have found that the older I get the more I realize that no one is going to work your field as hard you do. Nobody is going to push this music as hard as I am going to push it. There are different degrees of work ethics. My folks have always worked hard, so I have learned you get what you put in. Some will never work as hard as I do and be as hell bent to get to that next level. I find it easier to just treat it like a job where a band is involved. I have learned to keep a list of musicians. If one of them cannot make it, I move down the list until I find one who can. It is not easy finding a combination of badass and humble talented folks. When you do, hold on to them.

Professionals do not allow the show to be stopped just because their usual players can't make the performance. One that comes to mind is Jeff Ledbetter. He has no idea how much he has inspired me as a person and professional musician. I can never repay Jeff for everything he has done. You must have work arounds for every situation. There is nothing tougher than tension between band members even when we were a badass band. I hope those that I have had disagreements with over the years have found it in their hearts to forgive me as I have forgiven those that I had ill feelings about. I sincerely apologize for mine. I guess I tended to treat my career profoundly serious and unfairly took it out on others. I could have taken a better approach and a better delivery to explain where I stood. Bad attitudes and vibes can lead to equally bad outcomes. Attitude can often override talent. It is all about providing a good show and entertaining the fans. Lot of times the fans do not pick up on a bad note or wrong lyric. It is much easier for them to perceive attitudes. Never let them see you sweat so they say.

I am back full circle yet again. Where does that leave me in continuing to do it the Clay way; the one-man gang versus taking that leap into having a manager. I cannot help but wonder if a manager will push as hard as I push. A pal of mind in Nashville Troy has helped translate some of the lingo of a recent management contract. The contract simply offered too many interpretations, even though they call it a rough draft. I have even insinuated that I would have a lawyer review it. Troy has helped me a lot from a businessman's and friend's perspective, even taking time out of his hectic day to help me understand the contract. He is a great guy and his wife Dawn can cook great food. They invite me over for dinner when I am in Nashville. There are too many horror stories of artist being taken advantage of by those they entrusted to taking care of their business. I would even be as concerned if a family member was managing my career. Good or bad, it is just the way I am. It's just plain scary to turn over the reins even if doing so is the smart thing to do. With that being said, if the right agreement came along, I would take it.

I wish Maggie were here with me, but she should be in Myrtle Beach by now. She had just received the Teacher of the Year Award in Abbeville. She teaches history and is attending a ceremony at the beach. These conflicting schedules prevented us from being together.

After American Idol, my life has been like poking a stick in a fire ant mound. I knew my worth before Idol because I was playing every weekend. Now that I have all these new followers, I must exercise caution because so many new people are coming to my shows. Unfortunately, some people come to take advantage of you. Not fans, but people wanting a piece of what you have. They often have offers to tempt you after having been on Idol. Being an Idol contestant does not always work in my favor where bookings are concerned. I am trying my best to work ticket sales and be my own manager right now. When I do a ticket-sales show I am trying to identify my true worth in the market. There is no other way to determine this without tossing out a line and trolling the waters. When I perform in Elberton it is a no brainer. People know me in my hometown. Same goes for Dahlonega, Georgia and Greenwood, South Carolina. These are local markets for me. I have no idea how that equates to places like Charlotte, N.C. or even terms. This is something for me to be hashing through while driving, but it is just me and the Rodeo, so why not. I often refer to knowing my worth. This is just a term used by performers, a gauge for measuring what you can earn from performances in various venues. This is not an egotistical term as some might think.

Thinking about road trips, I have frequently traveled to Texas in the past year. In new markets I take what I can get. Sometimes this means only being paid small bucks in Texas. It is often tough to get or ask for specific pay if I don't know them and the venue doesn't know my worth and how I might draw a crowd. Competition is in no short supply. Even before my Idol experience, I tested the waters in Nashville and there were folks there that suggested I should be doing ticket sales. It is not just a matter of knowing your worth, it means you're collecting data on yourself, stats to support the crowds you are capable of drawing. Those references can be utilized to show other venues the true representation of your performance history and who is really following your music. Doing ticket sales is a valuable investment, unlike just setting up in a corner somewhere on the weekend and playing for a couple hundred bucks. I can do this anytime. It is guaranteed money, but this doesn't help advance my career.

I had someone once tell me that sometimes less is more when you are trying to launch a career. I interpreted that as me performing less frequently at the larger venues as opposed to the weekly mom and pop gigs as the path I should be pursuing. It is tough for me to swallow and adjust to this philosophy because of perception. It makes it look as if I am not as busy. It is much different than me playing over a hundred dates a year like I often do. Now, when I go out of the area to perform, the first thing I am asked is how many followers do I have in the area. The venues are interested in documented ticket sales. They don't just buy into the fact that when you get Clay Page for whatever price I do my best to deliver a memorable performance. Face facts. I am not a cover artist, at least not yet. The learning curve is steep and often an unsteady one. It can be filled with plenty of potholes along the way. This has already been a ten-year journey for me. It comes back to that manager decision I am facing, so it seems.

Man, how time flies when your brain is fully engaged. I am in North Carolina now. Everything in my life, like in anyone's life, happens for a reason. What is meant to be is meant to be. Unlike a song, I cannot rewrite the ending. I believe in prayer and in asking for guidance. Stuff that we go through down here is just temporary anyway. Living it the right way ensures our forever path later. I genuinely believe this and in God's chosen path for us.

Funny, I just keep digging up worms with no place to fish. It just hit me out of the blue that it was not just true love that led me to disband the band. I landed in the hospital about that time. This incident certainly fueled the fire. We were supposed to play this gig in Ware Shoals, but I had landed in the hospital just before the scheduled performance. One of the band members had booked the show. His name was on the booking instead of mine for a change. I was sick in the hospital with an IV in my arm and this created a bit of tension. I never miss a performance. This was something I could not control or remedy. I think it pissed off those counting on the band performing. The venue did not understand how this impacted me and how serious I am about playing, but it was unavoidable. My band member who had booked the show now got a taste of walking a mile in my shoes and how it can be a humbling experience, putting his name on the line when usually that burden falls on my shoulders.

Thinking back, I have been blessed and have had so many people influence my life. I worked for a waste management company in Elberton called Waste Away. The guys who owned the business, Tubby, and Zeb Worley, instilled a work ethic in me in addition to my upbringing from Mom and Dad. They both have worked hard. I give a tremendous amount of gratitude to my dad for making me understand the value of sound work ethics as well. Just coming for what I consider a middleclass upbringing and having experienced a home foreclosure firsthand in high school was an eyeopener. Maybe we were below the middleclass line and were just living beyond our means. At my age, I am living in a 480 square foot cabin on my Uncle Norman's property. I call it my tiny house. I can certainly compare this to living in Nashville paying well over a grand a month to lease a 900 square foot apartment. Letting this sink in now sure puts things in perspective. I would take this life over that hands down. It is idiotic and not the way a person should have to live stressing about bills.

Wow! I am here. I am in Charlotte. I cannot believe I've treaded down so many paths during this drive. With everything that has happened in my life and with everything that is happening, and what might be ahead, I feel at this point that I am 'Somewhere In Between' what destiny has in store for me."

Same Sad Song

Clay's drive from Elberton to Charlotte had been nothing he expected to experience. Obviously, his struggles over the direction of his career were heavily on his mind. Contemplating what he should do had been dominating his thoughts for quite some time. Nothing had prepared him for the events that had surfaced though. It had been all good, allowing him to relive and rethink events that had impacted his past. Alone, it allowed him the clarity to reassess these significant points in his life and career. With it surfaced a better understanding of events you often take for granted or merely sweep under the rug. Clay now had a better appreciation of what life had tossed his way. Sure, these were mingled with regrets for how he had handled situations and had treated many of the important people in his past. Maturity can teach harsh lessons, but if one is willing to open one's heart these can be rewarding lessons. Clay has a better understanding and grasp on these aspects now. As for the Charlotte experience, Clay recaps how it played out after he arrived.

> "I arrived at my Airbnb and boy how time had flown on my trip. I use an Airbnb because it offers a reasonable and affordable place to stay."

For you that have no clue about what he is talking about, Airbnb is an app on the internet that connects people who want to rent out their homes or rooms to people looking for someplace to stay and don't want the expense of a hotel. The company came up with its name from air mattress B&B.

> "Well, I guess my first stop will be McDonalds for a little chow after my drive. It is conveniently across the road from my Airbnb. On top of everything else I am struggling with a sinus infection in Charlotte, not the best situation for sure. After settling in for a short period, an open house was first on the agenda at the Monroe Crossing Mall.
>
> At the mall I was introduced to a few folks associated with the AMG organization. A few minutes later, Norman Greenbaum and his wife arrived. Norman had that 1969 hit, 'Spirit in the Sky' which he also wrote. I was introduced to

him. That was quite an honor. It was funny. After I arrived, I was off to the side just doing my own thing. I can be very introverted in these situations. When I was a kid, I was super shy. If I picked up on a weird energy in the room that I could not identify, I would crash immediately into introvert mode. This prompted me to be a bit standoffish in the current situation. It is not how I wanted to be perceived. I just could not help it. Being the only country artist in the field did not boost my morale for sure. I felt like the only hillbilly among other types of artist. This just contributed to feelings of isolation. No one made me feel this way. It is just a Clay thing.

The introduction to Norman and his wife broke the tension and eased me a bit. They were such cool people. They had this way of making me feel special in their presence. It was like I was supposed to be there and that I mattered. We struck up a casual conversation, including California and my take on going to Los Angeles during the Idol stint. I shared with them how I wasn't really taken with Los Angeles. I explained how I had really enjoyed the scenery from San Francisco to Santa Cruz though. That area had been one of the most beautiful places I has ever visited. They shared with me living in Northern California and the devastation from the fires there. As it panned out, I ended up sitting at the dinner table with them. Skip Martin and his wife joined us. Skip is known for being with Cool and the Gang. I remember that song in 1981 titled 'Get Down on It.' How cool was that, having dinner with Norman Greenbaum and Skip Martin.

Clay with Norman Greenbaum

Clay with Norman and his Wife

Skip Martin, Idol pal William Oliver Jr. with Clay

I was feeling out of place until then. I believe that they may have felt the energy I was unintentionally projecting. They perceived my awkwardness and made me feel otherwise. We discussed topics like Nashville, subject matter we had in common. It was a wonderful experience. Norman and his wife invited me to their greenroom and dressing room where we furthered the chat about the California wildfires. From Georgia, viewing the fires on television, while devasting, you do not feel the connection to what is really happening. Hearing the firsthand horror stories from Norman and his wife put a different perspective on it for me. I could feel their anguish and pain from what they had seen and endured. They were sincere, genuine, and down to earth.

Out of the blue, I started thinking about that kid in Calhoun Falls, and how we had picked on him and made life unbearable for him. It was just weighing heavy on my heart. So, what did I do? I felt compelled at that very instant to reach out to him. I did not know how to contact him, so I began fiddling with my phone and doing a search on Facebook. Low and behold, I found him. It was probably rude on my part, at the dinner table with these celebrities to suddenly burying my face in my phone. There was nothing for me to do but to reach out to him, so I did. I sent him a private message. I told him how I had been thinking about a lot of things recently. One thing had stuck in my head; just how we had bullied him when we were kids. I told him I wanted to apologize for my part in it. I added that I would have preferred handling this face to face but wasn't sure how to contact him. I just emphasized how I was sorry about everything I had done.

He messaged me back saying how it was a really nice thing for me to say, adding he would have thought I had forgotten about that after all these years. He told me that he loved my music and could not wait for more new music. To make me feel worse about how I had treated him, he shared with me how he had enlisted in the army later. I am thinking how we picked on him for being a little chicken and he does this. I told him that it takes a special man to have done what he had and join the military. I have a huge respect for our military men and women. I thought to myself that I could not have done that. This was a huge life lesson for me. It has taught me that it is never too late to make it right and to correct wrong doings in your life. It is wrong to disrespect someone because you never know when you might need that person in your life, or if they may need you in theirs.

Day one behind me. I returned to the Airbnb for what I hoped to be a good night's sleep. I had to be back at the mall the next day for an event mentoring kids. I was supposed to speak in front of them and share my journey thus far. I was experiencing a combination of excitement and anxiety. This is not one of my strong points, standing up in front of people and giving a speech or talk. It tends to play on my introversions that I am still trying to overcome for situations like these. It's funny. When I am wearing a guitar in front of a crowd, I don't react like that. It's a different energy. I am in my element. Without my guitar though, I feel naked. While the speaking in front of crowds is new to me it almost reminds me of when I first started. Walking on a stage wasn't the most comfortable situation for me. When I walked out in front of the crowd, I was trying to fight that crack in my voice.

Once I arrived, the kids made me feel better because they were super receptive to me being there. They appeared engaged in what I was saying and made me feel appreciated. Some of them asked me to play a song I had performed on American Idol, 'Die a Happy Man', so I obliged. Looking into those kids' eyes put things in perspective for me. It is tough to explain but I'll try and hope it doesn't come off as if I'm stereotyping the situation. You can tell the ones that come from the upper-class families and the ones that don't. I could pick the less fortunate out from the others because they would be the ones locked in, smiling, and enjoying themselves. The others were fiddling with their phones, appearing uninterested, and unimpressed. I have always gravitated to the underdogs.

There were kids in that room that I pegged as being the ones that had their fair share of struggles and challenges in life. I could relate because theirs were probably similar to mine growing up. In that moment I understood that music can be a powerful tool. It offers an avenue for kids that do not have a lot to turn to and the means to express themselves. It is something heartwarming to be able to share my story to all walks of life. There were photo opportunities with the kids and a time to sign autographs. My speaking stint lasted about ten minutes. It felt more like an hour. All joking aside, this time with the kids made my participating in the event worthwhile.

Friday did not have a heavy schedule; just some time allotted for sound checks. I ended up hanging out in Charlotte most of the day because we had sound check at four that afternoon. Some hiccups occurred and the sound check didn't happen at the auditorium. Norman Greenbaum was a true professional and took any inconvenience in stride. This offered me time to reconnect with some of my fellow American Idol contestants. Some may remember Shayla Wynn. She is legally blind. Her rendition during the tryouts of 'Rise Up' brought Lionel Richie to tears. She was eventually cut and did not make it to the final twenty either. Another was Drake McCain. He sang 'Eye of the Sparrow' during Hollywood Week. He was cut too before the final twenty. William Oliver was there as well.

It was interesting hearing and swapping stories of our lives after American Idol. We discovered we had traveled similar paths and had experienced the oddities, good and bad, from competing on Idol. This made me feel that maybe I am not quite as crazy I think I am. Don't get me wrong. I am still crazy but I'm not the only one feeling this way after the Idol exposure. As enjoyable as the Charlotte event was, I had hoped to drive to Powdersville and spend some time with my grandma. Instead I ended up having to book another night in Charlotte.

The main show was scheduled for Saturday and the sound check had been rescheduled for early that morning. I missed Maggie and I missed being home, but it was a rewarding experience even with the bad timing.

Clay with Idol pals Shay Wynn, William Oliver Jr. and Drake McCain

That brings me to the performance part of this adventure. I thoroughly enjoyed it. I encountered a first though. I had never read from a teleprompter. This was interesting and an eyeopener for sure. I performed two original songs that were scheduled for the November release on my new album. I sang 'Down Home' and 'Same Sad Song'. The crowd appeared to enjoy them. These were songs I had written. I began with 'Down Home'. It's an anthem about being proud to be from a small town. Something I have learned from all the recent travels; there's no place like Elberton, Georgia. As the cliché goes, there is no place like home. I would say that the only comparison for me might be traveling down Hwy 1 on the San Francisco coast to Santa Cruz. This drive is unbelievably beautiful. Most large cities feel empty to me. With as much as there is to do in these bigger cities there is just something missing; maybe my perspective from being raised in a small town.

I wrote 'Same Sad Song' in 2013. The first two lyrics of this song go something like this,

> 'I woke up this morning, put them shoes on my feet. Went down to the café to get me something to eat. I can get too much Lord. You know I got to eat cheap.'

Ironically, this fit my weekend adventure. It is a bluesy song. I could feel the energy of the crowd feeding off it when I sang. I received wonderful feedback for this one when I came off stage. It was not my typical country tune.

Several were amazed by my guitar playing. I told them I started out as a guitar player and have played for sixteen years. The singing came later. I will be the first to admit it, I was probably the weakest link vocally to compete on Idol. The others were blowing the roof off the place. Grammy award winner Reginia Belle performed for the Charlotte event. She is best known for singing the main theme song in Disney's Aladdin. She blew me away. That lady sang like an angel, perfect everything. All the performers were phenomenal. I was battling sinus gunk. That did not help a country boy from northeastern Georgia who doesn't have a huge range in the first place. I was doing my best to entertain with every ounce of talent I have. I give my all anytime I perform.

I was heading back home after the event and I phoned my grandma. We talked about a wide gambit of subjects as I drove. She is a good listener and gives me wonderful advice most of the time. We talked about where my career was and how the week had transpired. Regretfully, it wasn't in the cards for me to stop by her house. I drove straight home instead. I was just ready be back. Home sickness gets the best of me every time. In summary, this North Carolina trip had been a self-evaluation and appreciation week for me. It was mingled with a few trials and tribulations though. I'll just leave it at that."

Pure Country

Clay is indeed a true testament to his small-town country roots. To use Clay's favorite word, he hopes this is not a *stereotypical* segment. He often refers to himself as a country hillbilly. He is not ashamed of these stereotypes. His life is what it is, and he says he would take nothing for it. Small towns have their perks. Clay phrases it, 'Nothing beats living and growing up in Elberton, Georgia.' He also treasures those wonderful times he has spent in Calhoun Falls with his grandparents. His dogs, hunting, fishing, and just plain craziness have contributed to his life before music inspired him to change directions. Clay explains how it was in this era of his upbringing.

> "One of my favorite pastimes has always been riding four wheelers. I really wanted to be a dirt bike racer when I was a kid. I guess that Big Wheel stint kickstarted this ambition. I think the Big Wheels and bike riding happened around the same time. I stuck to my convictions if anyone asked. Nobody was going to convince me otherwise. I was going to be a dirt bike rider. Like most kids, I loved riding bicycles too.
>
> I honestly believed that I was the greatest person that had been destined to ride a bike. Sounds cocky, I know, but back then that is what I thought. I accomplished everything possible during my wild bike riding days. After completing my bicycle faze, I moved on to be master of the skateboard. As bad as I wanted a dirt bike though, my parents would not buy me one. I had to settle for a four-wheeler. They insisted that dirt bikes were just too dangerous. Finally, they caved and allowed me to have one when I was around nine. I was the coolest person who walked the earth then. I had blown up my four-wheeler and somehow, we were able to trade it for a Honda XR80. This put me on top of the world. It was a used bike but in good shape. It was my dream come true regardless of its condition. Proof is in the photos.

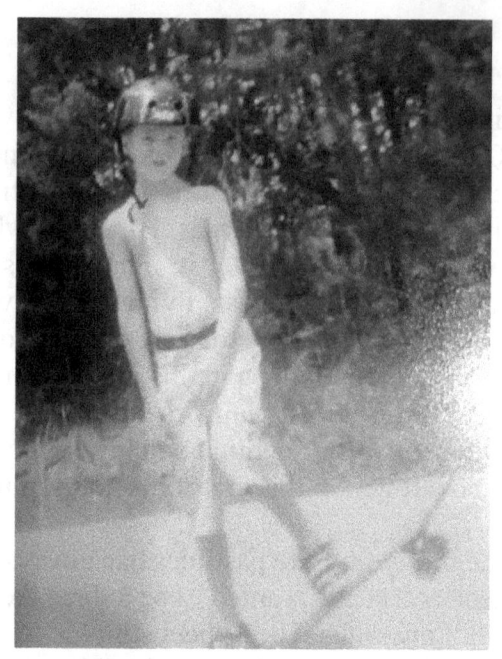

I had this Golden Retriever, Bailey, that used to follow me everywhere. Bailey was notorious for following when I was riding my four-wheeler. Everyone still talks about that dog and how he used to run behind me. Granddaddy would always say, 'Boy, that dog is going to have a heatstroke if you keep running him behind that four-wheeler.' Bailey was my best friend growing up. We spent a lot of time together. I never will forget how Mama and Daddy had gotten that dog for me one Christmas when we used to have our Christmases at my Papa James. He lived in a house just down the road from us. They had Bailey in a box. I was maybe five years old. Baily was with me until I was around seventeen. I was in my full George Straight cowboy faze when Bailey died. I have a picture taken of Bailey and me on the porch. I had a fishing rod in one hand as well. Fishing has always been in my blood. Living near the lake just fueled the fishing bug.

Back to Bailey though…this is a tough one for me to relive. I loved that dog. Mama did not believe in having inside dogs back then. We were not allowed to have pets living inside the house. As Bailey's health was fading and he was close to passing, she brought him inside. That was a shocker. I remember that night when there was nothing left to do but for her to take him to the vet in Royston, Georgia. to have him put down. He was crying and hurting so. It had to be done. This is breaking my heart all over just thinking about it. It is tearing me up sitting here looking at my other two dogs thinking how this is going to be a sad day when it happens to them. Mama loaded Bailey in the Tahoe and took him to be put down because she did not know what else to do for him. He was in such pain, whining, crying, and hurting. I remember how white faced he looked. As she handed Bailey off to the vet and he was placed on the table, he passed on his own. I was a wreck for a long while. At that time, losing him was the worst thing I had ever gone through in my young life. I had a few coon dogs then, but none were close to me like Bailey. Uncle Norman and I used to coon hunt, but Bailey was my buddy, my best friend. Back then there was a difference between hunting dogs and dogs that are real family. Oh man, these are some tough memories. I loved that dog."

Clay fights back tears. True dog lovers can appreciate his feelings. An episode like this forever haunts those who have had to endure the loss of a pet. Bailey had been his companion, his best pal for twelve years; a dog who had not dropped from heatstroke chasing along behind that four-wheeler. Like everything and everyone, we don't live forever. All we can do is cherish that blessed time shared. Clay's good memories outweigh any bad ones.

Clay with Bailey

Clay continues, looking at the dogs he has now, calling them his babies,

> "Remi and Lilly are looking at me like they sense my grief. I just pulled a stick from Lilly's throat a few minutes go. She was choking and I was freaking out. My granddaddy and I were working on a project placing underpinning on my tiny house when I noticed she was acting sick. It appeared like something was wrong either in the roof of her mouth or back of her throat. She was pawing at her face. She then comes over and nudges me wanting me to do something about it. I am panicking thinking she has swallowed something, and it is lodged in her throat. She appears to be struggling to breathe. What am I doing? I am looking at my cellphone thinking I should probably call 911. I told my granddaddy that I did not know how to help her. Nothing else to do. I finally stuck my fingers down her throat, not sure if what I was doing was helping or doing more harm. Somehow, I got my fingers on this stick lodged there and removed it. Boy, I thought I was going to lose her."

Clay with Remi and Lilly

Recovering from his pet episodes, Clay moves onto one of his favorite pass times.

> "Hunting can play on you too. I used to hunt every weekend before this career took it out of play. Back then I would hunt anything in the woods. I hope no one takes this the wrong way because I might come off as a softy tree hugger instead of the true country boy. As I have gotten older, I have transformed into someone that can hardly think about hurting animals, any animals. Now if I go hunting it must be a clean kill if I make a shot. My folks have always told me that I would be in serious trouble if I ventured into the woods killing animals just for the fun of it. There was not a squirrel that I killed that didn't end up on the dinner table. Mama always told me that you don't kill anything unless you plan to eat it."

Clay expands on the topic of hunting and some of his most memorable adventures.

"I have never killed what I consider a bragging size deer until last year. I did score a small ten pointer. I have always hunted mostly on what we call Corps of Engineers land near Lake Russel. My uncle and my dad have leased land for hunting though in Calhoun Falls. That might have been some of my best deer hunting days. There were acres and acres of prime hunting land. I thought it was a hunter's haven. They were so organized that the tree stands were assigned numbers. You might be hunting the #3 stand or the #7. The box stand was always my favorite spot. It was no more than ten feet off the ground. It was comfy and safe. It came equipped with a chair. I have a fear of heights, especially in a deer stand. I think the highest I have ever been in a deer stand is around sixteen feet. I was in it but on shaky legs.

It is confession time again. My fans and friends are going to think I am a big sissy. There was a time when I could not shoot my 308 Daddy bought me without wearing earmuffs. Let me clarify. I was maybe nine years old. The gun was so loud I wore the earmuffs all the time. I remember thinking it was a 22 and Daddy telling me it was a 308, and I was upset. We had shooting lanes cutout for the deer to cross. These had been clear cut, bush hogged. I remember one morning I was hunting in the box stand. The biggest deer I have ever seen in my life was crossing that lane in the creek bottom. The rack was huge. Instead of me taking aim and shooting the deer, I scrambled to get my earmuffs. I could not get them on fast enough. By the time I had, the deer had cleared the shooting lane. I was too much of a 'wus' to shoot that 308 without them. After missing that deer, I cried about it and never used those darn earmuffs again. Tough lesson learned for an eleven-year-old. It made for a bad experience and plenty of teasing. Mama would always follow up by saying, 'Poor deer, poor squirrel', etc."

**Clay with Ear Protection
Locked and Loaded with a Squirrel
for the Dinner Table**

"My buddy Jimmy Jones and I used to coon hunt all the time. I don't coon hunt anymore. I don't believe I ever could go now. It is brutal hunting. I didn't see it this way back then though. It is not humane, having two or three dogs on one raccoon. That part of it I sincerely regret but it was some of the best memories I had with my Uncle Norman Robinson. It was nothing better than being in the woods and hunting with him. Uncle Norman was serious about coon hunting. He had grown up hunting and had always owned coon dogs. Hanging out with him naturally encouraged me to take it up as well.

I will share a little insight into Jimmy Jones and what a character he was and still is. He had gotten this old dog from somebody and had named it June. Well, truth be known, June didn't do much of anything, especially when it came to hunting coons. I think that dog was good for just walking around in the woods, not much else. We had followed the dogs who were on the trail of a coon. Jimmy and I had gotten to the tree first. Uncle Norman's dog, Blue, had treed the coon. That old Blue Tick hound had struck the coon and had treed him too. When Uncle Norman arrived, Jimmy pretended like June had treed the coon. Oh my gosh! Jimmy picked up June and was telling her what a good coon dog she was. We were bad about pulling stuff on Uncle Norman. He never did but he should have kicked our butts. He was pissed, flat mad about the audacity of us saying Jimmy's dog had treed the coon. He told us, 'You know damn well, Jimmy, that your dog didn't tree that coon.' He really knew better but that is just how we were. We enjoyed keeping stuff stirred up and picking on each other.

Uncle Norma had a 1984 Nissan Datsun truck. He has passed now though but that old truck is still here parked on his property. During this hunting trip Jimmy and I were sitting in his truck waiting on Uncle Norman to return. The Datsun was bad about running rough, sputtering badly that night. I don't think he paid more than a few hundred bucks for the truck. He always complained about it being the biggest hunk of junk he had ever owned. Still, he drove that truck for thirteen years. I learned how to drive in it, my first straight shift before driving an automatic.

Getting back to the story…Uncle Normal kept this old jack in the bed of his Nissan. Boys will be boys and the two of us were quite a devious duo. We got the jack and then covertly jacked up that old truck about an inch off the ground. He returned and fired up that truck shifting through several gear and the truck was not moving. Jimmy and I were sitting in the truck beside him about to bust a gut. He was hot, fuming that the damn thing would not go. He had even shifted it into reverse, and nothing was happening. We finally could not hold it any longer and busted out laughing. Once he figured what was going on, he told us we better get that damn jack from underneath his truck.

Another night Jimmy and I were hunting with Uncle Norman and he was looking for the dogs. Uncle Norman could not hear too well and had bought this hearing aid contraption. He would hardly ever wear it though in public. He would wear it when hunting. He was touchy about people knowing he wore one. He wore these cheap versions from Wal-Mart. He would wear them so he could hear the dogs running.

**Uncle Norman Robinson with Clay
at a Jam Session at Swede's**

Clay so enjoyed those times coon hunting with Jimmy and Uncle Norman. It was not so much about the hunting as it was the fellowship and foolishness. You could tell in his voice how much he missed his Uncle Norman. He recalled another hunting tale, this one with his pal Tyler McKellar and Tyler's dad, Jeff, and Uncle Norman.

> "One night we were hunting near Beaver Dam Marina. Well, we had not started out hunting there but when coon hunting the dogs end up in places you didn't expect to go.

They just follow those sneaky coons all the while the coons are trying to lose them. We may put the dogs out miles away from where they end up going and treeing the coon. This was one of those nights that they ended up far away from our starting point. Tyler and I were sitting up on a bank on one side of the road. Uncle Norman and Jeff were standing on the other side of the road. A Beaver Dam Marina sign was in sight just up the road from where Jeff and Uncle Norman were standing. We found an old bottle. I told Tyler to watch this. I threw that bottle at the sign as hard as I could. I hit the sign making the loudest noise. Jeff hit the ground and Uncle Norman was still standing there looking at Jeff, as if asking what? He was not wearing his hearing aids and hadn't heard the thunderous sound that had sent Jeff looking for cover.

Tyler and I were bad about sneaking off and getting into something. His daddy is going to kick our butts if I spill the beans too much. Tyler used to slip cigarettes from his daddy's pack. We would sneak off from Jeff and Uncle Norman when we were hunting and light them up. We were teenagers doing what teenagers are supposed to do. Coon hunting was just somewhere different for us to act crazy. I guess I hunted about most everything back then but turkeys. For whatever reason I never got into turkey hunting. What I really enjoyed and still do is fishing."

Jeff McKellar earned his wings while this book was being penned.

Jeff McKellar
December 28, 1966 – April 22, 2020

Jeff McKellar, 53, of Elberton, GA, husband of Regina McCall McKellar, died suddenly Wednesday, April 22, 2020 at Elbert Memorial Hospital. He was born in Elberton to Wanda Bonds McKellar and the late Howard 'Buddy' McKellar.

Many happy hours were spent golfing at the Rocky Branch Golf Course, where he was a former member. Jeff also enjoyed fishing and cheering on the Georgia Bulldogs to victory. Most importantly, time spent with family, especially his grandchildren whom he adored, was the essence of his life.

Jeff is survived by his wife of 31 years, Regina; a daughter, Hali McKellar McConnell of Elberton; a son, Tyler McKellar (Corbin) of Bowman; his mother, Wanda, of Lowndesville; two brothers, Scotty Bonds (Shannon) of Greenwood and Bojo McKellar of Lowndesville; two sisters, Missy Blackmon of Calhoun Falls and LaFayette McKellar of Lowndesville; five very special grandchildren, Mylah Brooke McConnell, Brylen Kade

McConnell, Raelan Nicole McConnell, Karsyn Irene McKellar and Kolton Groves McKellar.

Clay's passion for fishing was shining through. Like with hunting, there are those unforgettable fishing tales as well. Every fisherman has a whopper or two to tell. Clay had his fair share. He laughed and decided to start with a lake story, not necessarily a fish related one. This was another one of those boys will be boys, unforgettable episodes.

"I'm guessing Jimmy and I were around fourteen when this one happened. We had just gotten out of our skateboarding faze and were on the verge of taking music a bit more seriously. Jimmy's daddy had taken us to Calhoun Falls. There we had bought some fireworks. After all, it was near the 4th of July. The summer had been extremely dry. The last thing Jimmy's daddy, David, told us before we got out of the truck was not to shoot the fireworks near the woods. Of course, we told him we wouldn't. We decided to go to the lake and test some of what was supposed to be waterproof type firecrackers. We had to cure our curiosity and see if they would explode in the lake. We were walking along and tossing firecrackers here and there. A spell later after returning from our lake adventure, we were walking up the hill and I mentioned to Jimmy that something smelled like it was on fire. He shrugged it off saying we were just smelling the powder and smoke from our hands. I get home and I'm in the bathroom at my mama's while Jimmy is in the other room playing on the computer. I could see my granddaddy from the bathroom window. He was stretched out running across Mama's yard as fast as I have ever seen him run. He knocked on her door yelling that the woods were on fire. The fire was on the Corps of Engineers property. I am hoping the statute of limitations will protect me for confessing now.

The woods were on fire and the fire was moving in the direction of a new house that had just been built. Jimmy and I were freaking out but keeping our mouths shut. Granddaddy had all his hose pipes stretched out, fighting the fire. He had mother's stretched and in action as well. A neighbor not far away had done the same. Everyone was pitching in and were battling the blaze until they had finally put it out. Jimmy and I let on like nothing had happened.

We decided to venture over to Broad River later that night and distance ourselves from the fire event. Avoiding admitting our guilt was not the best decision but we were teenagers in fear of the reaction by adults. David, Jimmy's dad, and a bunch of other people had a big party going on at the river. They were playing music and jamming. The fire had been extinguished so our worries were behind us. I could not have been there more than 20 minutes when Mama shows up. She lit my butt up, having somehow figured we were the perpetrators of the forest fire. It was a long time before I got that one off my back, deservingly so I must add.

Maybe it is best that I stick to fishing stories. They might be less incriminating. My buddy, Tubby and I were fishing a place people referred to as Twin Lakes. I worked for Tubby and his brother Zeb at their waste management company. Tubby would take me fishing to these two ponds. Usually we fished the upper pond of Twin Lakes. Often though he talked about the fishing in the lower pond, but we had never ventured there. I'm not sure why. Well, finally he insisted that we should give it a try, claiming there were larger fish to be had there. I was pumped and excited about trying out this alleged honey hole. We made the trek to the other pond, taking his molded plastic bass hunter boat along. He had a trolling motor mounted on the back.

Tubby was right. The fishing was excellent. We quickly caught a ton of fish. None were braggers but fish are fish. I had hung my line a few times, fishing a Texas rig with a zoom cherry feed worm on it. I tossed my line again, one of those impressive casts, feeling like I had tossed it 200 yards. I then became preoccupied with shooting the breeze with Tubby and forgot about my cast. I had let it sink to the bottom. Probably a couple of minutes passed, Then I noticed my line had started moving, the worm obviously resting on the bottom. I set the hook on what I thought must be a fish, but something didn't feel right. I turned to Tubby and told him I must be hung up again. Hardly out of my mouth and the line started moving a second time. I set the hook again and then the biggest fish I had ever seen jumped out of the water. The entire time I am reeling that fish in Tubby is yelling, holy shit, holy shit over and over, nonstop. It felt as if he must have shouted that 200 times while I was battling the fish on the other end.

When I finally got that son of a gun up next to the boat, we could see just how impressive it was. I brought that fish home remembering what my daddy had always told me; if I caught a fish as large as six pounds, we would mount it. This one weighed in right at six pounds, so we did. A fellow in McCormick, S.C. mounted that big mouth bass for me. It is a beautiful mount and is on my wall to this very day. And to think, I was just hanging out with Tubby, shooting the breeze when it happened."

Clay smiled thinking back on the great times he had with Tubby when he was fifteen, sixteen years old. His dad and mom were divorced at this juncture. He believed 'Tub' realized that he needed some guidance and mentoring in his life, given the circumstances and his young age. He was a teenager reacting to his parents and doing the opposite of what they wanted him to do. He was the common ground for Clay, the moral compass he needed. Clay reflected about his younger brother who is sixteen now. He expressed how he should spend more time with Connor like Tub had Clay. Connor is at that age where he could probably use some guidance as well so reflected Clay.

Even today, he and Tubby do not go long between conversations. Clay knows all he must do is pick up the phone and give him a call. Tubby is always there with a shoulder and feedback to assist Clay in working through any problem he is willing to share. Tubby is around fifty years old. He and Clay will forever be friends. He has learned a lot from his mentor. Clay also credits his mom, his dad, Nanny Camelia, Papa Ricky, Papa James, and Uncle Norman for shaping him into who he has become. You can tell a man by the company he keeps, and the lessons learned from those positively impacting their lives. Clay gives credit where credit is due. All wonderful thoughts. Clay casts his line into another fishing memory.

"I used to have a 14' Jon boat that I bought from Emmett Balchin in Elberton. It could not have cost me much more than a hundred fifty bucks and came equipped with a trailer. I purchased a couple of small old motors from the Swap Shop. Papa James helped me get them running. Jimmy and I would fish the lake behind my mama's place, spending many summers fishing the coves on Lake Russel. We were dedicated bass fisherman and spotted bass were in no short supply. Lot of folks call them rock bass. If I ever get skin cancer, that is the reason why. Jimmy and I are both redheaded and fair skinned. We would return from a day of fishing and would resemble a couple of lobsters. It wasn't anything for us to fish a battery dead trolling those coves. Then we would have no choice but to paddle back home. We were fishing, so who cared about the consequences.

On the lake you can always sense when a storm is approaching. We were behind Mama's one afternoon fishing stumps. We could hear rain somewhere nearby. The skies had darkened on the storm side of the lake, what we called the Carolina side. Jimmy said, 'Man, don't you think we should head to the bank.' It was thundering a bit, but I told him I thought the storm was heading on down the lake and was going to miss us. I had not gotten those words out of mouth when the biggest bolt of lightning lit up the lake. It is a dang wonder we didn't get shocked. Of all times for this to happen, the cable on the trolling motor broke causing us to do circles in the boat while it was now pouring rain. That Jon boat has never moved faster, us grabbing the paddles and off toward the bank we went paddling literally for our lives. We landed the boat on the bank and hauled butt through the woods. The storm was so fierce that it had felled a huge tree in Uncle Norman's yard nearby. Famous last words, me telling Jimmy we were good just before it cut loose on us."

Like any told stories, one triggers yet another.

"During the summer while fishing for bass you usually fish fairly deep. It has something to do with their swim bladder, a concept that is above my paygrade. Supposedly the bass go deeper in the lake. I have been told that if you snag them off the bottom and reel them up, the fish have a tough time adjusting to the depth change. Upon release they tend to belly up. Bass fisherman have a technique for somehow deflating that swim bladder before they set them free. I do not do any of that, mainly because I don't know how.

Maggie was with me this past summer fishing and I caught a bass. Sure enough, it bellied up on me. I did not just want to leave the fish, so I placed it in the live well. I figured I may as well clean it and cook it rather than just waste it. We were doing more hanging out on the lake than fishing. We so happened to be nearby to an Osprey nest. Young ones were visible in the nest. I told Maggie that I was going to feed them the bass. There was no need to keep the one fish. The nest was on a pole in the water remarkably close to where we were drifting. Jokingly, I tossed the bass into the water. Within seconds the adult Osprey snatched it up and returned to the nest. Maggie and I were in awe watching this unfold before our very eyes. It fed the bass to its young."

Clay seldom gets to hunt and fish now, his demanding schedule and career aspirations taking priority. He admits he could often use the experience in the woods or on the water to clear his mind and cleanse his soul. Killing or catching something would be of little concern. Just being out there would be enough. He leans now toward his love of fishing rather than hunting. Having his two dogs over the past couple of years have made him a bit soft about having a desire to kill animals. If he had owned an aquarium it might have impacted his ability to fish and harm them as well.

Clay remembered the last deer that he killed, looking through the gun's scope and thinking the deer was not much different than looking at his dogs. Not having any venison in the freezer finally won out and he made the kill. Luckily for Clay, it was a clean shot but not an easy one. He was perched in a climbing deer stand facing the tree. The deer was almost behind him, over his right shoulder. Clay had to pull off an awkward shot, remembering a similar incident when the scope bloodied his eye. He recalled the largest deer he had ever shot being a small ten pointer, a basket rack. His dad had mounted it for him, a European style mount. Clay is not a sports hunter. For him it is all about putting food on the table.

Clay recalls the first song he ever wrote was named 'Pure Country.' This was during his full-fledged George Straight era. He had his country persona in full swing, wearing a cowboy hat and wrangler jeans when YouTube was just hitting the scene and being extremely hot. There was nothing for him to do but write the perfect country song and post the video. Clay started making videos weekly and posting them. This was huge for someone 14 years of age. He posted a music video of 'Pure County.' He describes it as being homemade as it gets. Clay belted out the lyrics.

We sat on the riverbank
And caught catfish
On a hot summer day.
And everybody in the community
Knew our names.
They said those damn old boys
They will never change.

Clay explains,

"This was one of my Uncle Norman's favorite sayings, 'Those damn old boys are never going to change.' Like I have said, we were always cutting up with Uncle Norman. When I began posting my videos a few people poked fun at me. Looking back now, rightfully so, those were not the best by any stretch. Kids would pick on me in high school because of them. What goes around, comes around, bullying wise. I was a target for wearing my wrangler jeans, being picked on something fierce. My peers did not appreciate or relate to the cowboy outfits I wore most of the time. That was fine. I always strived to be a little bit different. I would be lying if I didn't admit that sometimes it got to me. Nobody likes to be picked on. Listen to me now. I did the same to others when I was younger.

I was passionate about the singing and the look that accompanied it, so I did what I did. I thought, maybe they are right. Maybe I do suck but I was going to keep playing because I enjoyed doing it. I figured maybe one day I would be good at it. As a teenager there is no shortages of insecurities."

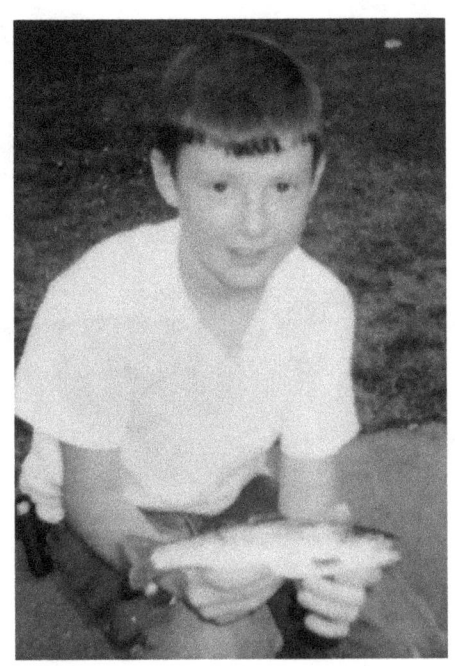

Young Clay the Fisherman

Friend Brett with Clay

Bailey with Clay

Clay with a Keeper from an Annual Trip with his Dad

School Daze

Clay exercised caution moving into this period in his life. Things were much different, not nearly as much politically correct scrutiny existing in a small town when compared to the national and world arenas. Folks accepted and tolerated stuff more then. Most didn't try to read something into everything someone did or said. His world was not filled with hatred and bigotry for the most part. Being politically correct did not enter his mindset, nor did it impact the thinking of most he knew. This was the south and the south did not get caught up in the craziness that others viewed as important and relevant. Living for the moment, having fun, and just enjoying life and those around you meant more than protesting silliness. Clay tells it his way, uninhibited, and uncensored with no ill will meant by his rhetoric.

> "In high school I was going through the cowboy stage wearing those wrangler jeans, rebel flags on my tee shirts, and thinking nothing of the meanings others tried to hang on it. My attire led to me being bullied. People who didn't understand me thought I was trying to make some sort of political statement, but I really wasn't. I was just southern and proud of it. I thought I was being cool. I never considered any political statements others might be interpreting by how I dressed. That just was not me nor how I saw things. This led me to writing a song about it titled 'When We Were Kids' and the lyrics went something like this."

> *Dixie Outfitters on our shirt*
> *Dressing like we did farm work*
> *Just trying to make a scene.*

"That's all we were doing. We were dressing like redneck-farmer cowboys. We were not trying to be what people THINK the rebel flag represents. We were not trying to appear to be racists or anything remotely to it. Our dressing in this manner had nothing to do with a black versus white thing. That never entered our thoughts. We did not realize then just how badly it offended some people. It was not our intension by any means. Looking back now, I can see it from both sides. Maybe it was not the best decision we made. I cannot change the past. It just happened. We were rebellious teenagers trying to find our place in the mix in a small-town environment. To me it was no different than me sporting earrings. It was the me shock factor. I was just trying to be cool and outlandish, nothing more. I guess it was my image, my perception of being a musician or punk, whatever you want to call it. Bands were dressing like this. We just followed suit. We mimicked for bad or worse.

Older now, I realize that there are good and bad people from every background and from every race. Where I am in my career, I never want to project the worst imagine. I am not perfect and never will be. I have a drink occasionally, but I am not going to allow that lifestyle to define who I am. That is not me. We all do stuff that we are not proud of. I have surely identified my fair share of regrets. I have tried to make amends and apologize when I could. I do my best to present myself and my career in a positive image. Same goes for carrying guns and hunting with guns. I grew up with everyone having gunracks in their trucks. None of us went on killing sprees. We respected guns and used them to hunt, nothing more. Thoughts of using them otherwise was not part of who we were; what many portray southerners as. I have already stated how my passion for hunting has changed as I've matured.

Vehicles were a huge part of growing up in a tiny southern town. I had modified catalytic converters on my truck. I probably had the loudest truck in high school and thought I was cool. It is funny now though. I cannot stand hearing vehicles with loud or no mufflers. I guess it reminds me of just how ignorant I must have been back then. I find myself cussing at one when it pulls next to me at a traffic light. It is funny how perception changes and I'm only twenty-five. That was me not that many years ago. I am watching my little brother in the yard cleaning the tires on his vehicle. Watching him babying his ride reminds me so much of me. What does the future hold for him?

No denying, I was kind of weird in high school. I had a few teachers that I liked. I always remained quiet and performed well in those classes. Then there were those few that I did not care for. I acted up in those classes and didn't do as well grade wise. Jimmy and I tended to lean toward being the class clowns in the classes we dreaded most. I was terrible in math. It has never been a strong suit for me. I think I failed math every year that I was in high school. This is not something, by any means, to be proud of, just saying. Algebra and trigonometry just were not my thing. They kicked my butt.

One year, Elbert County Schools were not being held on Mondays for some reason, but I attended those days to focus on math. This is shameful to admit but I used to cheat off Jimmy Jones's papers in class. Jimmy could cut up as much as me and still score a 100 on every test while I was making a 20 unless I managed to fudge from his. We had dividers between us supposedly to prevent kids from cheating. I had bored a peep hole through the one when I was seated next to Jimmy. I could often score 80s and 90s on tests then. Shameful, I know. I knew better but a kid must do what a kid must do. I had not developed morals.

Coach Smith, one of my teachers, tended to be a main target of my foolishness. We were awful in his class, cutting up, knowing no boundaries. This led to him separating me and Jimmy in class. Once I had been moved my math test grades plummeted from in the 80s to failing. He took note and told me, 'Clay, your grades have dropped since I moved you away from Jimmy.' My defense was a smart-alecky remark, telling him I had not been studying much lately. These are more of my regrets, part of my apology tour, being sorry for taking those shortcuts and now understanding the importance of school. Especially since my girlfriend Maggie is a schoolteacher now. I told Maggie that if she and I had attended the same school and she had seen how I acted; she would have probably never dated me. I no longer take those unethical shortcuts. If memory serves me, I crossed paths with Mr. Smith at the wellness center and I did tell him how sorry I was for acting the way I did in his class. I did not tell him about the cheating though. Some things are best left in the past.

Maggie did mentor me, helping me with math. Evenly more importantly, she helped me identify some of the issues I was having. I give her full credit for ensuring that I graduated. I surely could not count on the Jimmy crutch forever. I cannot pretty it up. I was not fond of the high school experience. I could have easily dropped out and spent my time playing music, hunting, and fishing.

I was working with Tubby at the time and thought I had everything figured out in life. I even had it in my head that my folks might sign the papers and allow me to drop out. Fortunately, I had a few teachers in school that did not give up on me, telling me to just hang on for one more year and then I was done. I am so thankful I came to my senses and listened. Tubby probably had some influence over me as well.

The foreclosure to our house really messed with me. It was very humbling and humiliating. It wasn't just tough on me; it was tough on my mama because she was doing the best she could to provide for us. I was not helping the situation with my terrible school antics. I was burning the candles, playing music on the weekends, working some with Tubby while he was doing his best to guide me. I had the makings of the perfect storm, all the tools at my fingertips to doom me. Dark clouds could come crashing down at any moment, the perfect recipe for a disastrous outcome. Thankfully, I had good parents and other wonderful mentors to keep me focused on the positive aspects.

Clay's Home after Foreclosure

My FFA teacher, Michael Bilow must have seen through my punk persona. He wasn't buying the renegade sporting earrings and my irresponsible behavior, like blowing my duck call in class. Unexplainably, he and I became good buddies. The defining moment was when he called me in his office one time, evidently aware of the stuff going on in my life like the foreclosure. He looked me in the eyes and told me if I needed anything to let him know. He did this without bringing up anything. I have never forgotten that moment. This was so simple but so sincere. What an impact it made on me. I cannot thank the mentors enough, those responsible for keeping me on track.

I still consider myself as being blessed, not that it has been an easy road by any means. Plenty of kids have a much tougher time than I experienced. The horror stories are endless and breathtaking. My attitude has always been that whatever I am going through there are many others going through a lot worse than me. Life is all what you make of it. It will beat you down if you let it. You can feel sorry about it or do something about it. My family and I have had our differences and we will always have disagreements. It is just part of life. For me, it's how you grow and how you take those differences and turn them into something positive. Regardless to the circumstances I had towards my folks, I love them both dearly and thank them for pushing me forward."

Clay's school experiences are not necessarily unique in some perspectives. Kids struggle with their own demons, their own inadequacies, and encounter bullying or other disruptive forces. Peer pressure can doom the best of the best. High school is not always the greatest environment for those depicted as the underdogs. Like many kids living in rural America, Clay used to ride the bus while in school. Tyler, Jimmy, and Clay rode the bus together which didn't always work in favor of the bus driver. For first time riders a bus can be a bit intimidating. After the boys settled into the normalcy of the routine, trouble followed. Quickly the driver realized the urgency and necessity to separate the young riders for the journey to and from school. This became an annual August event, the separation of the three. It was for their protection as well as the driver's sanity. It worked in the driver's favor being one of Clay's neighbors, assisting in the preparation of best laid plans. Mischief is not uncommon among youths, those with oats to sow, and an endless supply of energy and overactive imaginations. Clay left it at that…what happens on the bus stays on the bus.

Positive mentoring can often make or break the situation. Clay has been fortunate to have been surrounded by so many positive influences in his life and to have possessed the fortitude to heed their guidance. Older now, he appreciates those values instilled in him along the way.

"There have been times in my career when it has been tough and easy to give in to them. Backsliding can surely come into play. I try to shake the cobwebs and not fall into something that cannot possibly improve the outcome. Too many singers or artists fall into drugs and drinking when life is not going their way. This is no way to deal with situations. There can be a fine line between something like social drinking and crawling into a bottle. I have thankfully avoided the destructive paths many have chosen as a means of coping with the unfair circumstances they have encountered. I am no saint. I will just leave it at that. I try to project positive energy and represent my brand the same way. I do not want the final chapter in my life to be that of a loser, a drunk, or junkie. My thing lately has been if I have a bad day, the last thing I want is a drink. I try to have that be a toast for when I'm celebrating good news, not coping with bad."

Clay gets back on track with another high school memory, thinking about how he was this skinny 130-pound soaking wet rebel without a valid cause.

"I was skinny as a rail throughout high school. That was another issue I was very self-conscious of back then. I have gotten into fitness to try to change that image now. All the football jocks were lifting weights and beefing up. I was not into it then. I was still that social outcast. I never possessed the jock mentally of being on a football team. I thought about lifting weights, but most had the perception in high school that if you did not strive to play sports, you couldn't do something like lift weights. That was reserved for the dedicated athletics.

I was always self-conscious about my size. After I graduated and was no longer under the peer scrutiny. I began working out. Weight gain has not been an issue since high school. I am regimented now and go to the gym at least four or five times weekly. Even something as simple as my posture is critical to me. With my transformation people often come up to me and ask if I played football in high school. It's funny how people peg you based on how you look. The football clique would never have allowed me to hang out with them. I was too much the rebel, wearing outlandish clothing.

I chose to hang out with the rednecks. I drove an old hand-me-down Ford 150, a gift from my granddaddy. Scrap metal was big back in the day. I would haul off scrap metal in that old truck for a little pocket cash. I might use the money for buying speakers for my truck one week and for tires the next. My senior year I was working with Tubby as much as I could and even giving guitar lessons at Stan's Music World in Elberton for a little extra cash.

With all the craziness and being a social outcast, I managed to be voted most likely to become famous in my graduating class. By that time people began taking notice of me because of my music. It had nothing to do with me being popular. It was because my music was growing, and people were seeing me play at various venues. I guess looking back now, I was walking around poking out my chest like some of those jocks, just in a different way. I didn't have muscles, so I expressed myself with loud music and a loud truck. Funny how I perceived them as appearing to be the big dogs and in my own way, I was doing the exact same thing. They were the big dogs and I was a skinny dog, each striving to be popular in our diversely unique ways.

I eventually graduated with a class of three hundred. I think most of us became tight those last few months of school. We were almost like family. Guess it is part of growing up when you are at the end of those school days. Even the people who picked on me had let up by then. I have said this before; it doesn't pay to cut ties with anyone. It is part of that never-ending growth process. I have found myself in this forgiveness sequence of my life, forgiving people for how they treated me and asking forgiveness for how I have treated others. Bullies, the bullied, ex-girlfriends, and friends, I forgive them all and hold no grudges. I hope the feelings as life goes on are likewise toward me."

Pictured left to right in 2004: Clay, Hunter Blackmon, Tyler McKellar, Jet Totter and Jimmy Jones

Clay with Bentavious Allen

Tyler McKellar, Dylan Alexander, Clay, Hunter Blackman and Dre'kevious Huff

Jimmy Jones, Hunter Blackmon, Tyler McKellar, Clay, and Jet Trotter

Clay fast-forwards this conversation as it relates to where he is now and how he believes his family sometimes perceives his journey and experiences. He begins with Camilla his grandmother.

> "My grandma and I have had this very conversation recently. How can I not forgive somebody when I have been forgiven? God has forgiven me. I am saved. I am a Christian. The key is projecting forgiveness to others. We must all learn how to forgive. This includes forgiving yourself. When you really take the time to wrap your mind around that, it is something magical. The losses of loved ones the past couple of years have really opened my eyes to this. Life is too short and too fragile to be pissed off at people. How can anyone have hatred in their heart when that energy can destroy you? I am not projecting myself as a preacher or saint because I'm neither. I find that I am constantly self evaluating and trying to figure out how I can be a better person. My Grandma Camilla has told me that sometimes I try to be an idealist and focus on everything being right all the time. She has pointed out to me that life isn't going to always be perfect. I have a tendency when my life is not as smooth as I would like it, to allow it to hit me hard. You must see the good in every situation. Sometimes it isn't easy, but you must be willing to try.
>
> Being in this business can be quite complex. I do not always feel that my family understands the stress I find myself in when trying to make things work. I need to work on the way I deal with my frustrations. Sometimes I can speak harshly that I don't believe they care about me and what I'm dealing with in my life. I shared this with my grandma and admitted to her that this is a selfish way for me to behave. It is not that they don't care. They aren't doing what I am doing so it is tough for them to relate to what I am going through. Realistically, it is no different than them dealing with their jobs, coming home to me telling me stories that I might not understand about their situations. Everything is relevant.

Sometimes you say things you do not really mean, or you struggle to word them the right way. When they have been spoken it is impossible to take them back or pretend that they didn't happen, especially if they are hurtful. This year has been filled with a boatload of self-assessment. Sometimes undergoing the self-evaluation process and worrying about what others think can interfere with my growth as an artist and musician. I can forget who I really am."

Southbound

This segment in Clay Page's journey begins in Georgia as does most roads. We will begin at Randall Shirley's home. Randall had a home recording studio in Bowman, Georgia. Clay had been doing some recordings for a while. His mom had bought him a USB microphone. His first recording though had been at high school in a computer class. Some of the boys had invited him to use it and record some music. That lit the fire for young Clay. He picks up the story from here.

> "Randall Shirley was the first person I had ever seriously recorded with other than the stuff I had been doing at home and that one time at school. I must have been sixteen. I had known Randall for a while from performing live shows. He performs or performed with the Lazarus Unwound group. One of my guitar players had told me about him having a home studio. We decided we would go over and cut a few songs. I cut maybe four songs there while I was still in high school. I furnished the CDs and the CD covers. I then burned copies from my computer. I sold them at several gas stations and other places in Elberton and elsewhere for maybe five or so bucks. The CD had five songs on it. This was when YouTube was still hot and going strong. I was making plenty of YouTube videos then. People downloading tunes was in the beginning stages of iTunes. I researched and figured out how to get my music on iTunes."

Do you remember the names of the songs on the Randall Shirley recordings?

> "Pure Country was one. The album was called Pure Country. All were originals I had written. There were five songs on the CD: Pure Country, I'll Be Ok, Georgia Saturday Night, Loving on Me and The Shoals referring to Ware Shoals, South Carolina. I don't think he charged me a dime to do these recordings. He enjoyed doing them and so did I. If he charged me anything, it wasn't much. Sadly, I haven't seen Randall in two or three years."

Clay begins talking about a studio he later had in Elberton.

"I had a little studio in Elberton. Randall would come over and do a little work for me, playing the piano. Brad Evans, a buddy of mine, had a project with Randall as well. Randall is a super nice guy and can play the fool out of a guitar. I have bought a couple of studio speakers from him. I still have those speakers but hardly ever use them now. Those were the first speakers that I ever heard myself via a recording. Randell is such a great guy and is a good friend. I credit him as being an intricate part of my career."

How did your first studio evolve?

"This is a story within itself. I was living in town, just outside of Elberton, before I ventured to Nashville. I moved away from home at age nineteen and began renting a house in Elberton. I was not fond of living in the city, so I relocated just outside of town. I ran into one of the guys I attended church with. He owned a building with maybe just over 1000 square feet. We, Maggie, and my buddies, called it the fellowship hall because it resembled a church with double front doors. It resembled a place where a church might hold fellowship. It had one bedroom, one bath and a utility room in the back part of it.

Most musicians can relate to this statement; you cannot have enough equipment. We always must own the latest and greatest. I am no different. I was always buying more equipment. My bedroom ended up doubling as the recording studio as well. My bed occupied the same space with drums, an assortment of other musical instruments, speakers, my recording equipment, and my computer. The bedroom was also the utility room with a view of the washer and dryer over my bed's headboard. This was not the best arrangement, but it was mine.

About this time, Tubby Worley and his bother bought an old hardware store on the old Elberton Highway. The building had a display room as well as a garage and warehouse. We worked it out so that I could use and transform the display room into a new recording studio. That worked perfectly, freeing up my bedroom so it would be just that, a bedroom. My Granddaddy James Robinson pitched in and we worked on the studio project for about six months. I had drawn a layout of how I envisioned the studio. I wanted an area designated for teaching guitar lessons, a space for a recording studio and extra room for storing instruments. The finished project far exceeded my expectations. Without Papa James' help this would have never happened.

While we worked on the studio, I was involved in all sorts of things. I was giving guitar lessons, recording with my friends Brad Evans, Kevin Long, Elliott Satterfield, Randall Shirley, and Jeff Ledbetter. I miss playing with these guys. Brad was enjoying me being in the area as was I enjoying the same. I had gotten comfortable with the arrangement. That is a problem I have. When I become too comfortable with a situation, I have this mentality that kicks in telling me it is time to move on and do something new and different. Getting too comfortable almost freaks me out because I have larger aspirations for my life."

Nashville began eating away at Clay, tugging at his heartstrings. He started thinking that it might be time he gave the bigger picture a try. He began focusing on audio engineering role in the recording arena and less focus on his song writing and following his dream. Doing this and being a guitar teacher had quickly lost its luster. He finally confessed to Tubby telling him he had been praying on what was the right thing for him to do. Prayers answered. He had decided to move to Nashville to give it a shot. This move was not going to be a dropkick. Clay had to get his finances in order to make such a move possible. He bartered an expensive shotgun with his friend to make his dream possible.

This was Clay's springboard. The Georgia boy was finally heading for the big city in Tennessee, a place where many dreams have come true while others have sometimes been crushed. He ventured out of the fishbowl and now prepared to literally swim in the ocean with the much larger schools of fish. This was 2016. He had his mind set. Head strong and with much larger dreams on his mind,

Nashville was now in the crosshairs. Clay had high hopes but really wasn't sure what to expect. He had birthed this idea over a two-week period with no real game plan other than to get there. It had been a quick decision, yes, but his entire life he had seen himself doing this. Now or never, Clay takes the reins and share's his feelings and thoughts as reality now stared him down.

"I'm just a Georgia country boy. I finished high school but never attended college. My music had taken priority over my education. The Lord blessed me with this gift, this talent, and I felt compelled to put it to use. Leaving was not going to be easy. It was tough to leave the love of my life, Maggie. I was also leaving my family, friends, and two dogs to take this monumental plunge. I left, found an apartment in Nashville, and life as I had known it began a new chapter. This was possibly the biggest risk in my life. Moving there, I was overcome with the excitement of finally being where I had always dreamed of being. I'm here. I had arrived.

I called myself having done the research, following various songwriters' careers while back home. I was seeking out the places around the city where songwriters had made it. After I settled in, I would venture downtown almost every night. I would go to the midtown area. I stayed clear of what they called Broadway. It's the touristy part of Nashville. I focused on what I perceived as the hot spots. I would arrive and order a beer and use it as a prop. I would milk that beer as I tried to mingle and meet anyone that I possibly could that might have songwriting connections.

A week into my move I visited a place called Blue Bar and purchased my beer so that I would not appear awkward hanging out in a bar. I would observe the people who appeared to oversee the rounds of songwriters entertaining on stage. While small talking with the bartender, he pointed me to a gentleman. I strolled over and introduced myself to a man named Patrick Rains. He was hosting the Round. A Round consists of several songwriters taking turns singing the songs they have written. I told him who I was and that I would be interested in participating in one of the Rounds

> one night. He gave me his contact information saying he would keep in touch. The Blue Bar ended up closing, but Patrick and I stayed in touch."

Clay stuck to this routine, heading downtown at night, and trying to meet contacts. Many of the individuals hosting the Rounds are well known in the circuit. Finding a reputable one to hook up with became a priority for Clay. Exposure in Nashville is the key when seeking support and a potential career. Being involved with a set of songwriters in Rounds was a crucial component. Picture a group of musicians sitting on stools on stage while taking turns performing and seeking the reaction of the crowd. More importantly, who might be in the audience checking out the talent. Clay explains.

> "Many of these places are very intimate settings. There is a low tolerance for people being disrespectful while the artists are performing. It is nothing for them to call people down if they are being disruptive. I met a gentleman one night named Rob Snider who hosts one of my favorite Rounds in town. Revival was the name of the establishment. I had watched Rounds at Revival back in Elberton. It was a huge experience when I finally had the opportunity to play there. People who usually performed there made their breaks in the business. People with careers often hang out there and perform just for the heck of it. This remains one of my favorite places. If I am in Nashville on a Tuesday I try to attend.

> One of my goals for moving to Nashville was to become a songwriter. I figured others were there to cut a record deal. When I arrived and pursued this direction, I quickly discovered that I had been sadly mistaken with my assumption. It was the complete opposite. More people were vying for songwriter opportunities. I was the little fish in the big pond for sure. Nashville was instead a songwriter's town. This was quite the humbling experience. I have heard songwriters performing at the Revival that were nobodies that had just moved to town and they would knock your socks off.

> Competition was in no short supply. I realized quickly that I had two options. Jump in there with these guys and try to make a name for myself or go back to Elberton. The phenomena inspired me. I had the attitude that I was there to do the same thing and try to make a name for myself. The cool thing about this is that other songwriters hang out at the songwriter rounds. It's a network."

Clay was in Nashville for more than a year. He remained focused. He now had a plan, a dream, and was determined to make it a reality. Reality can bite the best of them, yet he remained relentless in his pursuit, like a bulldog with a bone. That does not mean that there weren't challenges at every turn. Clay explains.

> "There were nights that I didn't want to go downtown. I would find myself missing home and becoming melancholy. I had to convince myself that I didn't move five hundred miles away from home to just sit in an apartment. I would suck it up and go. Some nights I could walk into a place and ooze confidence. Then there would be those nights that home was weighing heavy on my heart. I was missing Maggie or thinking about my family, and dogs. I might be pumped up over some good news or stuck in life's pits. I still forced it even when I didn't really want to go. It is funny though how more times than not, those nights I didn't want to go ended up being the best nights. I'd find myself making contacts."

Clay fast forwards and talks about meeting David Lee Murphey at a gym. For those who do not know David Lee Murphey, he's an American country music singer and songwriter best known for his hit songs 'Dust on the Bottle' and 'Everything's Gonna Be Alright.' He has cowritten singles with other recording artists such as Kenny Chesney, Jake Owens, and Jason Aldean. Clay had begun working at a gym to supplement his income while in Nashville.

> "An eye opener for me was the cost of living difference between living in Elberton and living in Nashville. To survive in the big city would require finding a job while I tried to make inroads there. I had gotten into fitness back

home and had become certified in Les Mills Grit. It was a HIIT Class, HIIT is a group fitness certification, an acronym for high intensity interval training. My life before moving to Nashville had been to go the gym first thing in the morning for a workout and then back home for a shower. I would then grab a bite of breakfast and head to my little studio to work on my projects before teaching guitar lessons in the afternoons. I became an instructor at a local gym, Body Plex, where they paid for me to obtain the certification.

Needing a job in Tennessee I decided to utilize my certification credentials. I enjoy the gym environment and seemed a better solution to my needs. It is a great place to be around people and make new friends. I applied at YMCA and landed a job. Working in a gym came with challenges though. To make it to my assigned time I had to rise and shine early enough to be there by 5 AM a couple of mornings each week.

The early start to my days was extremely rewarding as I was meeting some great people. The flip side, it was gnawing at me. I had moved to Nashville with greater aspirations but found myself back into a necessary work grind. This was not how I had envisioned my Nashville experience. Chasing your dream does not come free. I was doing the early morning part time job and still hitting the night scene. This is not easy to balance. I am not complaining. I have always burned the candle at both ends to make things work while seeking a better life. I had not envisioned wearing a YMCA uniform while in Nashville. It was humbling. Thankfully, I enjoyed the gym scene. I tried my best to rationalize the experience as another steppingstone in my life and a way of solidifying my work ethics.

I met a guy, Bill at one of the gyms. Bill seemed to know everyone, and we quickly became friends. He told me that I would be surprised by who shows up at these gyms. You might meet songwriters, recording artists, and a variety of local celebrities. I had this personal peeve working out at the same gyms where I was employed. Once my workday ended, I was ready to leave. I just could not find the right zone to exercise in a place where I worked. I ended up going to a third gym for my personal workouts when I had extra time in my hectic schedule.

I was working out one day and this guy came in wearing a camouflage cap. It is odd because it is rare to see someone wearing camo at a gym. Something struck me as familiar. We exchanged pleasantries; how's it going and so forth. Then it hit me. This dude looked just like David Lee Murphey. To satisfy my curiosity I Googled him and sure enough, I was in the presence of the country singer. I decided not to let on to him that I knew who he was. I did not want to be pegged as someone there harassing or disrespecting him. Star or not, he has a life just like everyone else.

I began seeing him on a regular basis, several times weekly, at the gym, still not letting on that I recognized him. As bad as I wanted to introduce myself to him, I held back. I did not want to come off as a starstruck fan or a stalker. One day we ended up in the locker room at the same time and I decided to break the ice. I told him what a huge fan I was of him, someone I had always wanted to meet. He was receptive to my approach and we began talking for a bit. He asked me what I was doing in town. I confided in him saying I play and write and told him I worked a part time job at the gym.

We just made small talk a bit, the weather, this, and that. He shared with me that he had some buddies who lived in Georgia. After that we continued to see each other on a regular basis. As bad as I wanted to talk music with him, I bit my tongue. I didn't want him to perceive as wanting to take advantage of him and the situation. He had been genuine with me and I did not want to mess that up. I settled for enjoying his company and him allowing me into his world.

By this time, I had accumulated enough music to record a CD. I had met a few other songwriters and had written some new stuff. During a routine workout I mentioned to him to go to cut a CD. There is no shortage of studios in Nashville, like granite sheds in Georgia. I had the capability of recording my music and it sounded okay, but I didn't want to settle for just okay. I wanted it to sound great. I figured if anyone knew the best place to get this done it would be him. He offered several options, Oceanway Studios, or Legends Studio. I ended up going to Legends. I told them the cash I had available and asked what it might get me. They gave me their options.

At this point I am not digging Nashville like I thought I would. I am missing home. Uncle Norman was getting on up in age and I also found out that my Papa Ricky had cancer. Here I am away from them trying to chase this dream. My mind was in overdrive, but I started working on the CD. The day before I was scheduled to record the CD I was back in Elberton. This was not odd for me because, the entire time I was there, I traveled home every week while still holding the part time jobs in Nashville. While at home I would work local gigs to supplement my Nashville lifestyle. Out of the 14 months I lived in Nashville I can count on one hand how many weekends I stayed in my Nashville apartment. In Nashville somebody like me cannot make much money playing music, but I could back home. You can make good money if you play the Nashville Broadway scene but that was too touristy and no different from playing background music back home like I had been doing for ten years. Others might argue in favor of playing Broadway, but it was just not for me.

The back and forth was wearing me down, compounded by my family situations. I somehow continued to manage the chaotic balance. Thank goodness you can always count on family to lend a helping hand when it is tough to make ends meet. I put more miles on that Rodeo leaving on Thursdays and returning on Sundays. I had planned to head back on Monday because Papa Ricky's cancer was taking a toll on him. I was scheduled to record the CD on that Tuesday. I remember getting in the Rodeo in Elberton to head back and had this tug telling me I needed to go see him. He had contracted some complications and the cancer was not making it any better. I wasn't aware of the severity of the situation then. I know when I got in that Rodeo and shifted into reverse to back up and then shifted into forward, it hit me. Go see your granddaddy.

I had not talked with my Grandma Camilla that day. Everyone was aware that I had to record on Tuesday at Legends Studio. David Lee Murphey had recommended it and I was super excited about doing it. I drove directly to Greenville, South Carolina where Papa Ricky was in the hospital. When I arrived, my grandma was in tears. She was surprised I was there. I told her I had dropped by on my way back and would head in on Interstate 40 for a change instead of my usual Atlanta route.

She asked me if I had talked to my mama. I told her I hadn't. She then dropped it on me saying my granddaddy might only have a few days left. That explained the tug, but I was now a wreck. This was one of the hardest things I had ever done in my life. Faced with this recording session in Nashville tomorrow, I couldn't cancel it. I did not want to leave my granddaddy though. Decision made. I balled all the way to Nashville. I utilized the five-hour drive to process the situation to prepare for what seemed inevitable.

My buddy, Brad Evans was on his way to Nashville via the Atlanta route. This was going to be a big deal for both of us. Brad had written two songs that would be featured on the CD. I had invited him to Nashville for the event, a bit of a reunion and celebration planned. I phoned him and broke the news, telling him my granddaddy might only have a few days left. I wanted him to be aware because my plans had changed. I would be hauling ass back to Carolina after the recording session. He understood my priorities.

The next morning, Tuesday I reported to Legends Studio. I told Dan the engineer that I was prepared to work on it as much as I could. I explained the situation saying I was headed back to Carolina today. I asked him if he could send me a rough take of the songs so that I could take them for my Papa Ricky to hear. As we prepared to record the session, I noticed one dude through the doors that stood out from the bunch. I recognized him. It was Adam Shoenfeld."

Adam Shoenfeld is a professional guitarist, songwriter, and producer. Primarily focused on modern country music, his guitar playing has been featured on over 200 albums. He is strongly associated with Big & Rich, and Jason Aldean.

> "He was one of the A list musicians that were there for my session that day. I had informed Dan that David Lee had reached out to me and had told me to get in touch with him if I was going to work on the CD. He said he would come through for me and he had certainly made good on that promise. I am a firm believer that everything happens for a reason. God works in mysterious ways. Prior to our starting my session, someone on the crew commented that they had experienced a tough recording session earlier. That put a little fright in me, hoping I was not going to let them down as well. I put on the headphones and the guys hit the first downbeat and cord of the song. I slipped up and said a curse word unaware I was on a live mic. I was excited and it came through everyone's headphones. I knew then that this sound was what my music had been missing. There was no comparison to how I had been doing my recordings with that professional recording quality and talent. Nashville owned it. I have remarked several times in the last few years that I will probably never record and release stuff on my own after hearing this. Those bedroom recordings are a thing of the past."

Given the circumstances and his concerns about his Papa Ricky, I asked Clay how the recording session went.

> "It was phenomenal. Both Brad and I were blown away. As predicted, as soon as we finished, I hauled ass down the road. They sent me the recorded songs as I was driving toward Carolina. I get back to Greenville that Tuesday night and played the songs from my CD for Papa Ricky. After leaving the hospital I returned home to Elberton. The next day I was about to get in my car at the fellowship hall to head back to Greenville when I received the call from my mama that he had passed. I am so glad I returned directly to the hospital and he had been able to listen to the music from my **Southbound** CD before he died.

> This is the man who bought me that Isuzu Rodeo and the enclosed trailer that I still have today. As I look at the Rodeo right now it brings back the memories and tears. Papa Ricky played a huge part in my career. I cannot describe how devasted I was at the loss. This was a solid kick in the gut for me during my Nashville experience."

Clay was still hanging on in Nashville, waiting, hoping, and seeking that big break. So far, nothing had popped as he described it. He had met some famous people and had an incredible recording session, all notable, but he had not achieved his goal yet. Losing his granddaddy had taken the wind from his sails. He began questioning if he had spent enough quality time with him. Ironically, the emotional rollercoaster ride Clay had endured after hearing about his granddaddy's pending demise had somehow carried over into the recording studio. It had positively impacted his session producing an incredible performance. Papa Ricky Haggerty had contributed one last time to Clay's career.

Papa Ricky's pending death had inspired Clay's A game so that he could return to Carolina as quickly as possible to visit him in the hospital. He realized he had not been the most talented, given those who surrounded him in the studio, but it had brought out the best in him when it counted the most. Clay, to this day, will tell you he is not the most talented, but he has gained valuable experience. No denying it, **Southbound** had been inspired by Papa Ricky. Clay will be the first to say that there might never be another as special as this one. Clay picks it up again.

> "Through all this, losing him, the excitement of the new CD, working the part time jobs to make ends meet, back and forth to Elberton every week, I now find out Uncle Norman's health was declining. He too had taken a turn for the worse. Mama had a tough time working her job and trying to see about him while I was in Nashville where I was of little help. I was missing Maggie. I was missing my family and my dogs. Being away from Elberton was weighing heavy on my hear. On the upside **Southbound** had been released."

These are lyrics from **Southbound**.

> *"Traveler on a train headed southbound*
> *Nothing up ahead just another broken town*
> *Where the next stop lands only God knows*
> *He sees her face every time his eyes close"*

Clay, faced with yet another family crisis, remained in Nashville doing his best to pursue the dream that had thus far alluded him. Trying to stay optimistic he channeled his focus on CMA week in Nashville now approaching. Nashville would be buzzing with entertainers, songwriters, agents, and venues hosting an assortment of events. This was the place to be. Clay was hopeful something would land in his direction, that one break he needed to leapfrog to that next level. He was primed and ready and could certainly use a distraction to take his mind off home.

> "Patrick was someone I remained in touch with, one of the hosts for the songwriter rounds. I contacted him and asked if he had anything that he could put me on during CMA week. He informed me that they were doing this thing at the Loews Vanderbilt Hotel and told me he would love to have me there. I had been in discussions with a few publishers by then. After confirming that I would do the Vanderbilt, a publisher had decided to come out and watch me perform. I was psyched about this. My focus would be on him and doing what I could to make an impression.
>
> Maggie had joined me in Nashville for CMA week. It was an odd feeling playing at the hotel. I could not imagine someone saying they could hardly wait to go to Loews Vanderbilt to listen to music. It was just a hotel. I was apprehensive but what did I know. Patrick was hosting it, so I figured that should be enough said.
>
> Dismissing any concerns, I played my songs for those present to listen. I met with the publisher that had come there specifically to hear me play. I also met another publisher from Atlanta, Georgia. It made a bit more sense me playing at a ritzy hotel after I had made great contacts there. Who knows who might be in town staying at a place

like that? Sadly, no deals were sealed that night. A few weeks later though I received an e-mail from someone associated with American Idol stating that they had seen me performing at Loews Vanderbilt. They extended an invitation for me to audition for Idol in Atlanta.

I told Maggie I thought it might be some sort of scam. It was just tough for me to fathom the odds of something like this being true. I was debating as to whether I should commit to it. I was unsure if it was legit and if it was, was it something I wanted to do. I had not been a fan of the American Idol concept, thinking I would rather be out here paying my dues and earning my fanbase. I was more into practicing with a band and playing, earning it the old fashion way. Many people had risen to stardom on the show, but it just felt like a shortcut to me. I wanted to get there on my own merit."

Clay struggled to decide if he should give the Atlanta Idol audition a shot. He did not want to be pegged as some overnight success after having played for 10 years trying to make it his way. He consulted Maggie, trusting her instincts. She quickly told Clay that he was crazy if he didn't. After all, they had reached out to him. It wasn't like he had decided out of the blue to go try out at one of the Idol locations. She insisted that anyone who knew him, would know better how much work he had put into his career. She had given him that little push and bit of encouragement but still he was not quite ready to jump in with both feet.

He then talked with his friend, Rob, the host of the Revival Round. He and Rob had cowritten a song. Clay told Rob that if he decided to audition for Idol, he wanted to use that song titled 'Something' for the audition. Rob added that you must take advantage of promotional opportunities when they come along. Maggie and Rob gave Clay enough of a nod, intent on swaying him to at least consider doing it. It was Clay's decision ultimately though and rested squarely on his shoulders.

From Idol to Full Throttle

Clay finally committed to the American Idol audition in Atlanta. What did he really have to lose? He had to keep this under wraps though. No one knew what he planned to do except the good Lord, Maggie, and Rob. He had gotten permission from Rob to play their song. Clay had kept it from his parents and grandparents. For those who asked, he kept it simple saying he had a meeting scheduled in Atlanta. Clay arrived in Atlanta inflicted with the pink eye. For those who have never had or have never heard of pink eye, it is conjunctivitis, an inflammation or infection of the transparent membrane that lines your eyelids and covers the white part of your eyeball. It can be easily treated but is contagious.

"I arrived for the audition and looked like I was stoned out of my mind. Auditions were being held in this huge hotel in downtown Atlanta. There were maybe fifty people there, people walking around wearing American Idol badges. They were using a large hotel room for the auditions. The room was filled with big executive types from American Idol. None of the upcoming season's judges were present, just executives and producers of the show. I walked in and auditioned. Here I am with pinkeye. There were people auditioning ahead of me that were blowing the roof off the place vocally, and they were sending plenty of them home. Many of them had ranges that were literally insane, like those gospel singers that can do anything you toss at them. I am getting a bit panicky, wondering why I'm there, set to audition with my little bitty range and pinkeye to boot. Maggie was with me. We were both taken aback by what was happening.

It was show time. They called my name and I went in there to audition. I confessed before I started that I had pinkeye, so they would know I wasn't stoned or had been crying. The entire room got quiet when I told them this. I was then advised not to touch anything. I think I made them feel as awkward I was feeling. I performed a couple of original tunes, our song 'Something' included. I was then asked if I could perform any modern country songs, something they would know. That's when I played Thomas Rhett's 'Die a Happy Man'.

After I performed that song, one of them asked what I thought about Lionel Richie, Katy Perry, and Luke Bryan. I told them they were awesome. They then said I was headed to the next round. All I could say was, do what, no way? The next thing I knew I was signing paperwork to appear at Lake Coeur d'Alene in Northern Idaho for the celebrity round with those three judges present. This was crazy, an opportunity like this falling out of the sky from nowhere. I had hoped for a break and here it was. It was just what I needed to let me know that I was doing something right."

Clay back peddles, remembering when he was leaving the funeral home after making the arrangements for his Papa Ricky's funeral.

"I had been in Nashville the week before his death. I now was leaving the funeral home after making the necessary arrangements for his funeral when I see a message on Facebook from Adam Shoenfeld telling me that the next time I was in town he and I should hook up and write. I believe God played a role in this, something I needed at the time. Adam has played on about every hit record, has toured with Tim McGraw, and has been Jason Aldean's session guy. His wife Katie Cook hosts CMT. I am thinking what an opportunity and I've got the American Idol gig to boot. I am also envisioning that Papa Ricky was up there playing a role in this and making things happen.

To muddy the water even more tough; what should have been a happier time in my life with the Idol experience, I lost my Uncle Norman mere weeks before I began the Idol quest. I had lost two people who meant the world to me in a short period of time. These deaths had set the wheels in motion for me wanting to move back home. With the crazy year I had already had in Nashville, these deaths opened my eyes, realizing life is too short and to be away from the ones you love.

At the end of the day I know I still must work. I will always have friends in Nashville, long after I move back to

Elberton. I can always go back there for visits. Many of my new friends were very understanding of my situation. Others insisted I must tough it out and stay the course. My hats off to those who can, but I am just an old homebody. I love Elberton. I love my family and friends. Nashville was my dream. It was fun, always something I wanted to do, but the big city didn't have that small-town touch."

His thoughts returned to Uncle Norman and an event that haunts him literally. You cannot make this stuff up. The following was how it happened according to Clay.

"Let me talk supernatural stuff, things that have purpose but can't been explained and shouldn't be questioned. Uncle Norman had been in a nursing home for several months. He had been sick for a while but had basically given up on living. Prior to landing in the nursing home, he was involved in an accident, a fender bender. The family and I decided that it was not safe for him to be driving. He might be in danger of killing someone or himself while behind the wheel. We took that possibility out of the equation by not allowing him to drive.

As I have shared earlier about Uncle Norman, he refused to wear a hearing aid saying, 'I'm not wearing a damn hearing aid and letting somebody see me with that on.' He was just too vain to wear it in public. For many years he refused to get a hearing aid just like he refused to get dentures. He was old school, a simple southern man with no put on to him.

Uncle Norman's quality of life had deteriorated. He had outlived his wife and both his children. It seemed he had lost most of his family members to cancer and now he had hit a wall, He had all but given up on himself. He had every right to have given up before now but hadn't. He could have turned to drinking or drugs, but he did not. He was an old cuss who would always tough out adversity.

I was on my way back from my daddy's house in Elberton one day, heading to get a bite to eat at a little place called Clifford's. I had driven right by the hospital and suddenly I experienced another one of those tugs from above telling me to go visit Uncle Norman. I was starving but I heeded the tug and wheeled my Rodeo around to make a stop at the hospital instead. You must remember that the last time this voice spoke to me the voice had been right, and I had stopped by to visit Papa Ricky. A firm believer I listened this time as well.

I pulled into the hospital to check in on Uncle Norman. He and I were sitting there talking about a little bit of everything. Nashville, family, and friends. He was fully engaged and aware of the entire conversation. He and I were having a wonderful visit. I was the only one there at the time. He told me to go for the nurse saying he was having a tough time breathing. Fifteen minutes into my visit he just died. It sends chills down my spin reliving it. He was fully aware of everything and then, just like that, he was gone.

I was in shock. That tug and now this. I was in tears. I phoned my daddy and said, 'You're not going to believe this. I stopped by to visit Uncle Norman and he died while I was here. I had just been talking with him.' Indeed, he could not believe what I had just told him. We had not expected to happen like this. I had been directed out of the blue to stop by and see him. What are the chances of something like this happening without spiritual powers in charge making sure I do? I was dealing with another tragic loss to a love one. American Idol had come along offering me a needed distraction. I figured I might as well give it a shot."

Clay obviously had struggled with the deaths of Papa Ricky and Uncle Norman, but through it all he had committed to the next stage of American idol. Everything else, including his Nashville move would have to take a backseat. It was time for him to cinch up his breaches and put his game face on. An opportunity like this does not happen every day. He would be preforming in front of the judges this time, Lionel, Katy, and Luke and in of all places, Idaho. Clay describes the next phase in his Idol journey.

"I spent months in preparation listening to podcasts, anything that I could to prepare myself mentally and emotionally for Idol. I listened to artists' interviews, famous people who were talking about being famous, attempting to prepare for what might be expected to compete on this level. I quickly discovered that there was no way to really prepare for the true Idol experience. It would compare to nothing I had ever done.

The trip to Idaho had been the second time I had ever flown in a commercial plane. In Atlanta they asked me if I wanted to do my audition in Kentucky or Idaho. I could go to Kentucky any time, so I picked Idaho. We flew into Spokane, Washington. The countryside was like nothing I had ever seen. I fell in love with the beautiful landscape. Lake Coeur d'Alene Resort had to top one of the most beautiful places I had ever been. I was competing with hundreds of contestants. Realistically, I felt like a number there. I was required to take a 500-question test to make sure I was not crazy. I must have passed.

Now it was time for the audition. I remember just before I walked through the door, I was so tired from the flight and the time change. I was nervous but I went into this with no real expectations other than God was working it for me. I figured I wouldn't be there if He weren't."

The following is the transcript from Clay Page's 2019 American Idol audition in front of the judges, Lionel Richie, Katy Perry, and Luke Ryan. Let's frame the scene. Clay enters carrying his guitar, wearing jeans and boots, his numbered audition sticker affixed to his thigh, a broad infectious smile ear to ear, just proud to be there.

Clay,
    "What's up? Y'all doing all right?"
Luke,
    "We're doing good."
Clay,
    "Been doing any fishing?"
Luke,
    "The lake is not lending any fish."

Clay,
> "I'd like to bring my fishing rod back here one day."

Luke,
> "Tell us who you are and where you're from."

Clay,
> "I'm Clay Page and I'm from Elberton, Georgia."

Katy,
> "I like how you talk from the one side of your mouth. It's cool."

Laughing Clay responds,

> "Oh, thank you."

Katy,
> "Are your boots taped under those jeans?"

Laughing Clay says,

> "No, they actually come up to here," pointing to where the boots are inside his jean's legs.

Katy,
> "Luke's boots are."

Luke,
> "Not today. They're kind of tight, taking a page out of my book."

Clay,
> "Where does the tape go under there?"

Katy,
> "Around the ankle."

Luke,
> "It keeps the jeans from flaring out."

Clay,
> "Wow"

Katy,
> "You can't stand flared jeans, can you?"

Luke,
> "I can't deal with a flair creeping up on me."

Clay laughs,

> "When I stand up it's like I have high waters on."

Everyone gets a kick out of Clay's reference and burst into laughter.

Luke,
> "What are you going to sing today?"

Clay,
> "I'm going to do a Thomas Rhett tune."

Luke,
> "Okay then, let's hear you sing."

Clay performs 'Die a Happy Man' as the judges appear to be enjoying his rendition. Upon completion, Lionel, and Luke clap and then they begin their series of critiquing comments.

Lionel,
> "Country is not my wheelhouse, but I feel close to the area. I like the vibes. I love a storyteller, somebody who can start singing and you got me on the story. I'm listening to the story and there isn't a whole lot of hollering and screaming, just telling your story. The voice was just right on the money. I like who you are."

Clay,
> "Well thank you. That means a lot."

Katy,
> "It's cool. It's real country and I really like that. It's pure country like Luke would say. I like that."

Clay,
> "Oh, thank you so much."

Katy,
> "You got the twang coming out of me."

Luke,
> "Well, Clay, man you have a very infectious knack. It's like a perfectly not trying too hard delivery that is so gentle to listen to. You might be our best representation thus far." (Katy and Lionel chime in agreeing). "You are not the best country singer in the world, but you do not have to be. You're just making us hang on your every word. I'm sold completely. I'm fired up."

Clay,
> "That is awesome, man."

Lionel,
> "I'll go first because I was the one that discovered him first. Congratulations, it's a yes for me."

Clay,
> "Thank you so much. I appreciate it."

Katy,
> "Clay, it is a yes for me."

Luke,
> "I'm a big time yes. You're going to Hollywood"

Katy,
> "Georgia boy is going to Hollywood."

Clay retrieves his golden ticket and shakes hands with the judges who voted him to the Hollywood round, yelling as he walks away, "I'm going to Hollywood."

Lionel,
> "That's the whole package there."

Clay now in front of the camera for his solo cameo tells the producer,

> "Wow, I can't stop smiling."

The producer replies,

> "You literally can't stop smiling. You are grinning from ear to ear. I think that's great."

Clay's Audition

Clay with Idol Judges

Clay had gotten his golden ticket for the next round, this one sending him to Hollywood. It had begun as a chance encounter in Nashville that had now routed him through Atlanta to Idaho and next to California. A lot had happened in a short span, cutting Southbound, losing Papa Ricky and Uncle Noman. Now this.

Clay Punches his Hollywood Golden Ticket

"The audition had transpired in front of the judges in one take, just as viewed on television. I am still blown away by my first-time meeting any of them. When I had walked into the audition area, they had the lights shinning on them so bright that the makeup made them look unreal to me. I was taken aback in their presence. There must have been as many as fifteen cameras in the audition area."

How do you compose yourself with the cameras, the celebrities and everything else staring you down the barrel?

"I really tried not to think about it a lot. No denying it, I was nervous up to the point I opened the door and then it all just went away. I was there to play and perform. It had been more of an anxious wait."

Clay had won his ticket to Hollywood; now what?

"I'm thinking, what's going on here. This is insane. It is crazy to relive that moment now. I haven't watched Idol that much. I still could not believe it. I am going where? The toughest thing was that I couldn't tell anybody about it. We were recording this so far in advance and were sworn to stay quiet. Here I am with all this great news and I cannot share it with anyone. I go out to Hollywood and obviously, I have never been to California. There were 150 of us in this round. I was thinking, even if I get sent home during the Hollywood round, I was going to feel good about the experience. If I get sent home at least I have had an opportunity to play a song in front of Lionel Richer, Katy Perry and Luke Bryan. This alone was pretty cool."

I had read some snippets about Clay and his take on winner, Laine Hardy. I asked him to elaborate on this and his relationship with the 2019 American Idol winner.

"Laine is a super cool dude. I think American Idol got it right. He deserved the win. Laine was on the 2018 show, making it to the top 40 but I did not know that. I didn't even know who he was at the time we first started competing. I had not watched Idol in years and didn't really keep up with it. I just thought he was another kid auditioning like the rest of us. I didn't know how to take Laine when I first met him. I thought he was a bit standoffish and that made me back off.

He had a guitar and I had gravitated to him because of that, but his vibes had convinced me to give him space. Later in the competition I found out who he was and about his story. It then made more sense. Later he started coming around and hanging out. Things eventually changed. I figured he had a dry personality.

Laine and I just become buddies. We even had little jam sessions between the competition rounds. Laine phoned me when my audition aired to see how I was doing with everything. His taking time to do this spoke volumes about the type of person he really is. He is sincere, the real deal.

Before the Hawaiian round, Laine phoned me out of the blue. We had not talked in over a month. He asked me what I was wearing to Hawaii. He didn't say hey, how have you been or anything, just opened with asking me that. I told him I had not put much thought into it. Later we were in Texas preparing to go to the Hawaiian round. Some of us were standing around in a group. Laine comes out of nowhere and walks up behind me. He is like a ghost and can just pop out of thin air.

I visited California after American Idol and I reconnected with was Tyler Mitchell, one of the contestants. I reached out to a few others while there, but nothing came of those contacts. Of all people though, Laine, the winner took time out of his schedule while I was there to hang out with me. We ended up writing a song together. Laine is a standup man. I have not talked with him much lately. Maybe the last time was about a month ago when I was back in Nashville.

I never want to be confused with a person wanting to get something out of him just because he won Idol. I cherish his friendship too much to compromise it. I call him sometimes just to keep in touch and catch up. I enjoyed hanging out with him and jamming with him. I never want to be perceived as the type to take advantage of anyone. If I like you, I like you. I am proud of anyone who have made their way and has a career. I'm striving to reach the same goal."

And what about your Hawaii experience, given this was the round where you had been eliminated?

"It was fabulous. Laine and I were always sitting around jamming during Idol. He is a phenomenal guitar player. I had always been drawn to good guitar players. If you have never seen that side of him, I am sure you eventually will. By the time we arrived in Hawaii we were best buddies. There were 40 people left at this point. This really put things in perspective. Back in Hollywood there were so many competitors that were not what I call necessarily real. When we got down to the final 40 all that was gone. We were more like family. American Idol and the judges do a wonderful job culling those from the bunch. This group was genuine. I felt no awkwardness being around them. They were real people. We had a top 40 group text that we still have to this day.

I was remarkably close to going further. I was asked by one of the producers how I would feel if I was sent home in this round. I just responded that I was so excited to be there, beyond blessed. To make the top 40 out of all that had auditioned and competed, I had already won. I was not even sure why I was there. I had maintained this attitude the entire time, just grateful for each stage. I had mixed emotions about advancing and not winning. At some point Idol wants you under contract. I got out before reaching that phase for better or worse, who can say. Looking back now, my response could have played a role in the decision as to whether I continued or not. Who knows? I'm not sure what response might have triggered a different outcome, if any. I'm sure they have a certain image in mind and who can blame them for that.

I remember one of the producers attempting to get a rise out of me before a performance. Looking back now, maybe I should have gone for more drama. I was asked how it made me feel going out in front of all the people and if the song I had chosen was going to be good enough to get me to the next round. I told him I hoped so. I was trying to get in a zone, and he was trying to rattle me. My prep is just being quiet and avoiding the hype and drama. One of the cameramen stepped in on my behalf and I told the producer that I was fine."

Would you ever consider competing again on Idol like some tend to do?

> "If someone reached back out to me I would do it in a heartbeat. I don't think I would just take the initiative and do it again on my own. You never close any doors, but at the end of the day, I would not want my whole career based on Idol competition. Take Carrie Underwood. Her career has not been based on American Idol. Look how much she has accomplished. I used to watch Idol in the Simon Cowell days. I have a new respect for Idol after competing. The talent is real. Idol is fair for the most part. Reality television is what it is. Just like the music business, it is what it is as well. But to be completely honest, I have not had a television in at least two years. I am not a television watcher. When I was on Idol, I went to my mamas to watch it. My focus is on my music and my career, not television."

How was your life after the Idol experience?

> "I've learned valuable lessons about the Idol brand after competing on the show. Flaunting the 'I was on American Idol' card does not always work in my favor. Venues that are doing hard ticket sales can often care less about American Idol. I'm not bashing Idol by any means, but I have learned that sometimes that is the last thing I should tell venues or event organizers because many tend to size me up as just starting out or green to the business. On the other hand, for smaller venues it works great. They eat up the whole American Idol phenomena, many having watched as I auditioned and performed on the show. For instance, if I perform in Abbeville or Greenwood it's a big deal, former American Idol contestant. In Texas on the other hand if you cannot guarantee ticket sales it doesn't hold water.
>
> The Idol experience, while wonderful, has contributed to a chaotic year for me. Smaller venues prefer talking directly to the artist. Larger venues prefer talking with an agent or a manager. If you are not represented, you must be small

potatoes. Having an agent can elevate your status in their eyes. Maggie has done her best on my behalf to serve in that role, but she has a career and life as well. She isn't always available to serve in that capacity. That's the way it should be. We are both following our dreams, mine as an artist-songwriter, hers as a teacher. That puts it back on my shoulders. I am proud of where she is. She works her butt off and has wonderful work ethics. I believe in her and am so proud of her and what she has accomplished."

Digging in the Dirt

Digging in the dirt was my Granny Bowie's favorite thing to do. She always had a vegetable garden and plenty of flower beds. Even into her eighties she still loved digging in the dirt. Nothing made her happier than getting dirt under her fingernails and watching plants grow, bloom, and produce veggies. I thought it might be the perfect title for this Clay Page chapter. Here though, instead of physically digging in the dirt, I would be digging up any dirt that I could from interviews with family, friends, mentors, and acquaintances willing to share those special stories excavated from Clay's childhood, hometown. or places somewhere in between.

I had a chance to contact two of Clay's cousins, those same big wheeling riding partners in crime originally from Calhoun Falls. Clay had referred to himself and them as mean back in the day. Kids tend to be kids and what might appear cruel actions were funny or common day backyard antics in their world. I am not defending their actions. I have been there too. What's right and what's wrong can be a fuzzy line in the minds of children. Clay has regretted some of his cruel antics and has attempted to rectify them. Ricky is the older of the two brothers, now twenty-six. Drake is twenty-three. Let's see what Drake and Ricky have to say.

Drake still lives in Calhoun Falls and he shares a few of his memories. He said that growing up they got into their fair share of mischief. They had a couple of clubs, the Clay Page Club and another club named after the kid they were prone to pick on. This is the same one that Clay had mentioned and apologized to recently. The boys would basically toss out dares and if they didn't follow through with the dare, they ended up being in the other kid's club. Drake said the boy rode what he described as a little girl's bike, because it was so small and had what they perceived as girl's colors.

Once, they convinced this kid to ride through the water hole between Clay's grandmother's house and their aunt's home he got stuck. Afterwards he had to tell Carolyn, Clay's grandmother what had happened. He got in trouble for doing it. Of course, the boys stuck to their story and claimed they hadn't put him up to it. Drake and the bullied boy were in the same high school graduating class.

Like Clay, he regrets the way they used to treat him. He said that the boy had grown up to be a great guy and had served in the military. He was proud of him, saying, 'He fought for our freedom.'

One of their favorite pastimes was the three of them, Drake, Ricky, and Clay, venturing into the nearby woods to have paintball battles. Clay owned an automatic paintball gun while Drake and Ricky had what he called semi-automatic paint guns. On this one occasion, the Smith siblings had fibbed to their daddy telling him they would be playing baseball. Ricky and Drake concealed their weapons inside a bag with their baseball gear in the back of their daddy's truck. Their daddy smelled a rat. Before dropping them off he checked inside the bags and found the paintball guns. He let them slide though. Later the battle began, the Smith Brothers against Clay. Clay pulled off his best evasive maneuvers utilizing the tree line, running from tree to tree, and firing off shots at his adversaries. Sometimes this worked, other times it did not. Clay later convinced Ricky to wear a pair of goggles. This must have been a lucky hunch because Clay nailed him in the face.

Drake talked about them riding the big wheels. They would stage races or push one another to see just how fast they could go. Making others flip them was fair game. I asked Drake who he would say was the best big wheel rider of the bunch. He quickly told me that he was the best of the three. He added that he would like to think that he was the best at everything they did back then. I warned Drake that now I would have to ask the others the same question. He commented that Clay had always been big into music, not something he just picked up as he got older. He remembered Clay as a small boy entering school talent shows saying he could pick the hell out of a guitar.

Next up, Ricky Smith who lives in Lowndesville, South Carolina. Ricky recapped their times with Clay in Calhoun Falls. He backed up his brother's tales of shooting paintball guns and BB guns at each other. He told similar stories of bullying a little boy there. He as the others, regretted ever doing that now. Like cousins do, often disagreements happen, and it leads to fighting among themselves. The skirmishes were even, tit for tat for the most part. Then Ricky admitted he thought he usually won. He walked into this one, so I had to ask who the best big wheel rider was. I did not receive the answer I was prepared to hear. He credited Clay with being the best, saying he would ride the hell out of his big wheel. They had a go-cart that had no motor on it and Clay would make the Smith brothers push him while riding it. They used to race bicycles up and down a path to a neighbor's home.

Ricky brought up when Clay first began playing the guitar, they used to go to Vernon Brown's where Clay took his guitar lessons. The boys told Clay that once he became famous, Clay would let them ride on his tour bus. Both brothers were asked if Vernon was still around and I received the same response…they thought he had passed. Ironically, I had worked with a Vernon Brown and his wife Imogene at Flexible Technologies in Abbeville. I recalled him picking some. Surely there could not have been two Vernon Browns in the area. I asked Ricky if he played the guitar and he quickly said no. He did add that he and Drake had been in Clay's first music video. He didn't say what their cameo appearance had required them to do.

After conversing with the two brothers, I was glad I hadn't attempted to contact Vernon Brown. That might have placed me in an uncomfortable and embarrassing situation if his wife Imogene had answered the phone. Some time after the conversation with his cousins, Clay texted me saying he had seen Vernon Brown and he was willing to be interviewed. Now I envisioned the *Escape from New York* movie. Everyone who crossed paths with Curt Russell's character Snake Plissken would remark, 'I thought you were dead.' Vernon Brown was among the living after all.

On cue, I talked with Vernon Brown. He was indeed the gent who I had worked with for 20 years. He had retired from Flexible after 40 years. I shared with him the conversation with the Smith brothers and their thoughts about him being deceased. He laughed, saying a few years ago their life insurance company had contacted Imogene thinking the same thing, that he was dead too. Vernon was alive and well at eighty-eight years of age, adding he had been blessed with great health and had never been seriously ill or had ever been in the hospital. Vernon indeed remembered Clay taking guitar lessons from him.

How long have you been playing music?

"I'm eighty-eight now and I have been playing since I was about fourteen. I started teaching guitar in 1972. I have made plenty of money from my music playing. I had considered quitting work at Flexible one time to just focus on the music. The only reason I didn't was because I wouldn't have insurance if I did. I was playing four nights weekly and had 54 students I was teaching guitar the nights I wasn't playing somewhere while still working full time. I stay busy. If there is a dollar to be made, I'm ready to go get it.

In 1958 I bought a Fender guitar from John B. Lees in Anderson, South Carolina. I still have it and knew it might be worth something. My grandson lives in Nashville and he took it there to see how much it might be worth by placing it on auction. Well, I wasn't interested in selling it. I made that clear to him. I told him when it got to a certain point just take it off, figuring it might bring a couple of thousand dollars. It got up to 10 thousand when he pulled it. My grandson was told not to sell it unless someone offered 25 thousand for it. Supposedly they made very few of them, maybe less than twenty-five. That guitar has made me some money over the years. It is showing its age though. The body is blonde, and I have worn rough places on it holding it and playing it so much.

I used to play in bands over in Hartwell, Georgia on Saturday nights. I have been lucky and had good people playing with me. I had to remind them from time to time what they were supposed to be doing. We never went by a band name though. You had to be careful calling yourself this or that because another band might already have that name and have the copyrights on it. People can get sued for that. Sometimes they would call us Vernon Brown and his boys. Nobody could get us confused with anybody else called that."

What do you remember about teaching Clay to play the guitar?

"Clay took lessons from me about a year. He learned quickly. I wanted him to stay with me a little while longer, but he was anxious to get out and perform. I don't think he realized it at the time that he would be eventually trying it in the big time. I had a lot more I wanted to teach him. He was doing so well but dropped out. He has come back a time or two and we've played a little together, 30 minutes here and there.

He and a few boys over in Elberton started a band and began playing, one thing leading to another and they became popular. They were putting on shows in the area. They then had offers to open for headliners performing around there. Local bands were selected to start the show for the big names. I think Clay began liking the experience.

I have always played lead guitar and he was doing what I call cording it, playing what I call the flat top. Most singers don't do a lot of leading when performing. The band usually kicked it off for the singer. He could do some lead, but he didn't get fancy with it. I didn't know at the time that he was going to go as far as he has gone. I did not know him before he began taking the lessons. He lived across the lake from here over in Georgia. I knew his grandmother and his mother. His mother was a beautiful woman.

I heard him playing at places like the Calhoun Falls City Wide Yard Sale and he was good. I can tell you one thing about Clay; he watched the professionals and I could tell he had learned a lot by the way they acted on stage. They carried it out well. He did good. I will have to say that. He knew what he was doing. He is a good kid. I like him. Tell Clay hi for me when you talk to him next and that he can drop by anytime. He and I talked recently, and he wanted to drop by, but I was taking Imogene to a doctor appointment and couldn't meet with him."

In ending our conversation, after talking old times from our working days of course, Vernon told me he still had a truck that I remembered him having that now had 253,000 miles on it. The only thing he has replaced is the power steering. He said he wouldn't be afraid to drive it to California. Sound familiar? I'm thinking Clay and his Rodeo. It must be something about vehicles in that neck of the woods. They keep going like the Energizer Bunny. Like the truck, Vernon has always been blessed with good health and has enjoyed life. He added that he had worked in the cotton mill in the 50s in the weave room and he is the only ex-weaver left from that time in a company that used to employ 1100 people.

Best friends are forever. Where better to learn about Clay than a chat with one of his best, Jimmy Jones. Yes. This is the infamous Jimmy Jones, Clay's partner in crime for the great American fireworks fire on the lake near the homestead. And yes, he is the prankster accomplice, an Uncle Norman tormentor. Jimmy as mentioned, resides in Simpsonville, S.C. and is married.

Jimmy confessed that he might have had something to do with that unintentional fire. Some of his fondest memories were of coon hunting with Clay's Uncle Norman. First one, he confirmed the incident when he and Clay had jacked up Uncle Norman's truck while out one night on a hunt. Apparently, both were quite proud of this prank they had pulled on an unsuspecting Norman. Either Norman was too trustworthy of the little duo or he just accepted that they were out to get him and just rolled with the punches.

Jimmy recapped the dog story, the new one that he had gotten and had planned to groom for coon hunting. Sometimes best laid plans don't work as well as envisioned. Jimmy said the dog would not tree a coon but would instead sniff the woods looking to jump a rabbit. Evidently the dog had decided to take the easier route, no treeing required. Jimmy would do his best to pretend the dog was a blood-blued racoon stalker, but Uncle Norman quickly dismissed those notions saying it wasn't a coon dog.

There were many more episodes in the woods, so many that none would come to mind at the time of the interview. Sometimes they would climb atop Uncle Norman's house and lean over and knock on his door. Norman didn't hear that well to start with and when he checked, no one would ever be at the door of course. They switched off all his lights once while he was on the phone. Annoying stuff had no end to it. All joking aside, both thought the world of Norman. Hardly a time passed when they didn't walk up the long drive to his place and visit or take a ride somewhere with him. He added that you had to be careful though. When Norman took sharp right turns the latch on the passenger side door didn't hold and it would fly wide open.

Jimmy was with Clay fishing the lake when the ill-fated thunder boomer rolled in and gave them a real jolt of reality. Jimmy said he had told Clay at least 100 times that afternoon that a storm was coming but Clay was too interested in holding his ground and fishing. Jimmy said Clay had no valid argument. You could see it approaching. Clay said, 'No man, we'll just keep on fishing,' refusing to give Jimmy the benefit of the doubt. That comment no sooner out of his mouth, the rain could be heard making its way through the woods on the near shoreline. Finally convinced, Clay gave in and was going to pack it in. That's when their only means of mechanically navigating the lake let them down. The trolling motor would not start. Lightning began striking the water around them; the boys literally up the creek now with only paddles as their means to make it back home. Jimmy said he literally walked across water that day.

So, we talked fishing, what about hunting? Besides coon hunting they did some deer hunting occasionally. Duck hunting was another pastime and again Jimmy claimed Clay was a better duck hunter. He recalled duck hunting once behind Clay's house. Birds flew in and both took shots. As they were retrieving downed birds, Jimmy pointed over to the one he had shot. Before he could claim his prize, it took flight. Clay quickly rubbed it in about how his pal had nailed his bird. Speaking of birds, the two did plenty of dove hunting, often picking them off while they were roosting on the powerlines. Jimmy laughed saying Clay might mow down a crow instead of a dove. Jimmy did lay claim to be the better dove hunter.

Sometimes the two work out at the gym together, more spontaneous than planned. Often it might be a Saturday free. This is more than just working out though. The fellowship is utilized to motivate one another, often discussing life's challenges and stumbling blocks. Positive talk and input are therapeutic for the lifelong friends with twenty or more years of friendship, something that cannot be replaced. Goals are discussed and paths to accomplish them. I had to ask if Jimmy could take him in the gym. It was tough to tell according to Jimmy, saying Clay holds back a lot. He had just recently gotten back into the workouts, but he felt he could still match Clay pound for pound. He added that this might work against him and motivate Clay.

He reminisced about the days of playing together in the band. His dad had taught him how to play guitar. Often Jimmy and Clay would spend times at Clay's house learning and practicing songs off YouTube. He remembered one of the first songs that they had learned was Uncle Kracker's 'Follow Me'. Here are a few lyrics from that song.

Follow me everything is alright
I'll be the one to tuck you in at night
And if you
Want to leave I can guarantee
You won't find nobody else like me
I'm not worried 'bout the ring you wear
Cuz as long as no one knows than nobody can care
You're feelin' guilty and I'm well aware
But you don't look ashamed and baby I'm not scared
I'm singin'
Follow me everything is alright
I'll be the one to tuck you in at night
And if you
Want to leave I can guarantee
You won't find nobody else like me

Clay and Tyler McKellar

Jimmy reiterated how he and Clay were really into skateboarding in the day. They would be listening to music while they finetuned their skills on the boards. Then they would come inside afterwards, pick up their guitars, and begin playing the songs they had been listening to outside. I asked, as I always do, who was the best skateboarder. Jimmy gave that accolade to Clay, adding he was the top dog. Jimmy laid claim to being the designated film maker for most of the stunts. Attempting to give Jimmy his shot at the top of the hep I asked who the better guitar picker was. Again, he credited Clay. He quickly laid claim to him being the best fisherman, adding he would take credit for that all day. He laughed, stating the photographs never lie. Clay would always be sporting the smallest fish between the two of them.

Clay gives a lot of credit to Jimmy's dad, David, as inspiring him to be a musician. David Jones played with a local group called the Broad River Band. Jimmy recalled how many times his dad would have some of his old mountain playing buddies at the campground, jamming around the campfire. One of the members of the Lewis

Family, a gospel and bluegrass band, would often join them. Jimmy said he personally did very little picking now. Work taking priority. He is a mechanic at the Donaldson Center Greenville Spartanburg International Airport. Clay had said he was envious of his buddy's position. Jimmy added that Clay calls him frequently wanting Jimmy to get him inside to look at the planes, being that Clay now enjoys flying.

I asked Jimmy if he had any crazy or memorable moments from playing with Clay in the band. Jimmy said it was just cool playing with him, having chances to be on stage, and playing in front of crowds. The Clay Page Band had played just before David Allen Coe one time at the Hartwell Motor Speedway. Mitch was on the lead guitar and Cody Strickland was on the drums. This was a big deal, quite the experience, them still being in high school at the time.

They also played at Simpsonville's Freedom Weekend Aloft in 2012. Freedom Weekend Aloft was a July 4th Weekend tradition in the Upstate for decades and became the second largest hot air balloon festival in the nation. This was one of the largest stages and in front of one of the largest crowds they had played. Clay had gotten to meet country artist Jake Owens that day.

Young Clay on stage at Freedom Weekend Aloft in Simpsonville, S.C.

Jimmy was given his opportunity to spill the dirt on Clay. He said over the years they all had their fair share of dirt on each other. When they visited Calhoun Falls to play, they were always introduced by one guy during the City-Wide Yard Sale as the Georgia Boys or Backwoods Boys. He said the best way to get the dirt was to put them together in the same room. Stories always fly then. His wife and Maggie get so mad at them because they tend to tell the same 2000 stories over and over, them never tiring of telling them. Their audience does not share the same nostalgic sense. Jimmy remembered Clay taking lessons from Vernon Brown but had never met Vernon. After taking lessons though, Clay had performed in the elementary school talent show, playing 'Folsom Prison Blues' when he was in the 4th or 5th grade.

He and Clay had attended kindergarten through twelfth grade together. The first year in high school they did not share any classes, but they made up for that over the last three. Clay had described himself as a punk in school. Jimmy admitted that most teachers were not too happy with them, cracking jokes and being a disruptive duo. I told Jimmy that Clay had credited him with being the smart one in math class and how Clay confessed he had cheated off Jimmy's test. Jimmy chuckled, remembering how in math class they had boards (barriers) between students to deter the urge to cheat. Clay had found a way around it. Jimmy said Clay had ripped a hole in it and all he could see was Clay's eyeball peeping through, asking if he had any answers he could share. Their teacher had once called them out, pointing out to Clay that he found it odd how his grade dropped 20 points after he had moved him away from Jimmy. They gave their teacher a tough time, once stringing fishing line across the class, undetectable and kids running into it.

I asked Jimmy who had the loudest vehicle when they were in school. No hesitation, honor went to Clay. He had the loudest truck in Elberton. Jimmy was driving a 1990 single cab beat up Toyota truck. It was loud as well, only because Clay had convinced him to saw off his mufflers. This had prompted Jimmy's dad to be quite unhappy about the modification. Both took turns at being the bad influence, so it sounded. He said Clay always has good stories about his Rodeo.

Jimmy ended by saying the old guard was planning a vacation or reunion of sorts. The dirt would surely be shoveled around when this happened. Bones would be excavated no doubt. I would sure like to be a fly on the wall when this happened.

Staying on point, I chatted with David Jones next. I caught him after work as he prepared for a night of fishing. David, age 59, confirmed he had played with the Broad River Band for quite a few years, but it never became a career opportunity. He is a mechanic at the Lake Russell Dam. His passion is fishing preferring to fish stripers. He had just texted Clay to see if he wanted to join him fishing but hadn't heard back from him yet. Clay had recently told David that he hoped to fish more in 2020. Boy, neither David nor I knew how the wish would sadly come true later.

David recalls that Walmart was sometimes adventurous when he had his son Jimmy and Clay tagging along. He laughed about how those boys were tough, but all right. He claims he had kind of helped raise all of them. He recalled one incident at the big box store when he picked up a bow and pulled back the draw string and it made a loud noise. He took off quickly laying blame on the boys for doing it.

Kids are kids and young boys are young boys, but he credited them with being good overall. He added how they loved riding their bikes and that they would jump ramps and land in the lake. They were known to set the woods on fire, adding to the reputation of Jimmy and Clay already mentioned. David confirmed that the last thing he had told them before they had exited his truck, 'Do not shoot fireworks in the woods.' How would that turn out? Not so good! David said that Clay's entire family and neighbors had to fight the fire they had started.

Do you see anything in Clay back then that indicated he might someday be a musician?

> "He took lessons. One day his mama called me asking if I could help him. Clay could play but mostly played cords. About the only thing he was playing was Folsom Prison Blues. I told her I could help, for her to bring him over to the house one day. She did and I asked him what his favorite song was. I cannot recall the song, but it was a Hank Williams Jr. tune. I played and he commented, man, that wasn't hard. We sat around and played for quite a while. In the beginning it didn't matter what I played, he ended up playing it the same way, same tempo until I helped in developing his technique."

I told David that Clay had mentioned how he missed jamming with him and some of the other band members. One of the members he had mentioned was a guy named Swede. David had recently visited Swede, adding that he was now 75 and did not perform much now. He and others still picked at his house though. David enjoys joining some of his old friends and having a little picking session around the lake. David's home was near the river. Residing in Georgia now, David was born and raised in Calhoun Falls.

David talked about how proud he was of Clay, working hard and staying on the road. He added that Clay was one of the most courteous, nicest guys you could ever meet.

> "Right after Clay graduated, he had been working at Stan's Music in Elberton. I told him then that he ought to move to Nashville. It was the place to be to meet people. He kept saying, 'I'm not ready. I'm just not ready.' He would not go. I tried my best to convince him to go then but he wouldn't."

What did you think about Clay ending up on American Idol?

> "I had tried to get him to try out for Idol years ago. He had already won the Elberton Idol. I told him he should now try American Idol. He said, 'I want to be a songwriter.' I tried to convince him to take a chance at Idol, but he said, 'Nah, I don't want to.' Five or so years later there he was, on Idol. I am glad he went. He got to go to California and Hawaii."

What advice would you give Clay at this juncture in his career?

> "He's doing so well that I don't think I could help him. He does some good stuff, playing for nursing homes and the veterans. He is a worker on all levels. I don't think I could help very much now."

Can you offer up any dirt on Clay, something people haven't heard?

> "Well, he greased up the handlebars on my four-wheeler one time. My boy had my four-wheeler over at Clays and I had ridden over to pick it up. Before I had gotten there, Clay had greased up the hand grips. I tried to grab it to load it and it was a slick mess. I cleaned it off mine and then wiped it on Clay's four-wheeler. His Uncle Norman was there. I am sure he has probably shared some stories about Norman.
>
> Those boys, my Jimmy, Tyler, and Clay could get into about anything. Tyler lived half mile from me. Clay lived less than five miles away. They stayed at one of the houses

all the time. His mama told me, 'You beat him up, he's yours. I told her that I knew how to handle those boys. He needs a whupping. I said, 'I've got this. I could handle them.' My daddy raised me hard. He is a great kid. Clay will call sometimes asking me how to play a certain song while I'm out on a golf cart somewhere. There I am trying to play the song in my head and teach him the cords on the song while he's trying to play it."

Ending the call, I told David I hoped he caught some fish.

"Thanks. We're going for a big one tonight."

Clay talks about David.

"David lives at Broad River and is employed at the Richard B. Russell Dam on the Georgia-South Carolina border. He played with a local group, the Broad River Band. David Jones was a singer for the group. I have had some special times with those guys growing up. They call themselves retired now but I had the opportunity of playing with them many times. Larry Snow, a guitar player, moved back to Kansas. He and his wife, Judy, are the sweetest couple you could ever know. When I had my studio in Elberton, they recorded some songs there.

Swede Sorenson was a bass player in the group. Swede is one of the funniest guys I have ever known. He is from Florida but sounds like he originated from New York. He must be at least seven feet tall. He always wears a New York Yankees baseball cap. He has shoulder length blonde hair. He straight up has that New York slang down pat. Blurting out the phrase sonofabitch is pretty common.

Swede bought a Marshall guitar amp from me when I was fourteen. He really liked the distortion on it. Distortion is the effect the amp has on the guitar. I had not thought about it in a while. He had it and kept it in his music room and used it when the Broad River Band practiced. When they did their so-called retirement, he dropped by my house and gave me back that amp as a gift. I had originally kicked myself for getting rid of it; maybe a $100-$150 amp at the time but it was my first guitar amp. He probably knew it meant something to me and gave it back. He has also given me a couple of base guitars. He brought me a 1960-something Fender base guitar. I have it in a case.

I learned so much from David, Swede, Larry, and his wife Judy. Jimmy and I picked and played with them. This might have been where the fire was first lit for me; there and between performing at the Calhoun Falls Town Wide Yard Sale. Playing was so much fun back then. I look back now on those days and miss just sitting around and playing music with them. If I ever have the time to just sit and jam with somebody, I jump on it. It's refreshing to do this and not be Clay Page the aspiring musician. It doesn't matter if I sing or not as long as I get to play a little bit of electric guitar. I so love doing that. It's a wonderful escape from being a performer on stage.

Back to David though. He is such a cool dude. His Facebook profile probably still has a picture of a big striper-bass on it. David used to get so aggravated at our shenanigans. I remember going with David, Jimmy, and Tyler when David purchased his Toyota Tundra pickup truck. This was before any of us had driver's license. We would ride in the back of the truck all the time after he bought it. While David was at the Toyota dealership in Anderson, we decided to walk over to the Tractor Supply Store. Tyler and Jimmy were bad about picking on one another. Tyler was inside the bathroom stall. He was wearing shorts. Jimmy found a horse whip in the store and began cracking that whip on Tyler's legs while he was still seated inside the stall. Tyler was cursing Jimmy for all he was worth.

David still owns that truck. I can remember riding in the backseat listening to David's CD collection. Some of the music that inspired me was from his 70s music. He would play Steve Miller Band, Marshall Tucker, Van Zandt, Lynyrd Skynyrd and Steve Earle music. My dad listened to this music as well like Steve Earle, but he was more into the rock style of musicians like Kenny Wayne Sheppard,

Creed and Nirvana. I got plenty of inspiration just riding around in David's truck.

Jimmy and I used to go to Walmart quite a bit with David. Our routine was to run away from him while we were in there. He would be ready to go but we would still be hiding from him. We had run away from him so much that he would go to the front of the store and have them announce on the store's intercom for us to report to the front of the store, our ride was leaving now. We still would not come. He would be furious. We were just kids, but it was a long ride back home from Walmart, with nobody speaking a word in that truck.

We have had some adventurous times in Walmart. Years ago, not sure now, but they used to sell bows and arrows in there. Jimmy and I were goofing around with the bows. David came by where we were. We were too scrawny to pull back the strings on the bows; too may pounds of pull for us. David said, 'Let me show you how to do it. Let me see one of them, boys.' He pulled that son of a gun back and when he released it the string slipped from his hand. It sounded like a gun going off in the store. I think people in the store were ducking thinking someone had fired a gun. David quickly placed the bow back on the shelf and yelled, 'Oh crap. Run.' We laughed until we hurt about David doing this.

I catch myself thinking about these times quite often. Jimmy lives in Simpsonville but I still live where all this stuff happened. Jimmy recently bought a house and is doing well for himself. I am tickled to death for him. Jimmy is smart and a hard worker. In school we could both cut up in class and Jimmy could still make an A on a test that I would flunk. I felt sometimes that I paid closer attention than him but still failed.

I am jumping all over the place, now thinking about Tyler McKellar. Tyler's mom and dad owned a store named Savannah Grill when we were kids. Regina, Tyler's mom, operated the grill on Bobby Brown State Park Road. Tyler grew up at this location. Jimmy grew up on Ernest Brown Road, just off Bobby Brown. Uncle Norman went to Savannah's every morning for breakfast. This was always my opportunity to ride with him. If everything worked out, he would allow me to stay there and hang out with Tyler and Jimmy.

Regina would be operating the store while Tyler's dad was off working his construction job. The three of us were a bad recipe, always into something. The lake was walking distance from the grill making it easy for us to do a little fishing and maybe things we had no business doing. It was the perfect place to grow up as far as I am concerned.

Regina eventually closed her place at this location and moved to the main highway for a while across from the boat ramp on highway 72, in what used to be Tony's Bait and Tackle. She relocated the grill a final time to Calhoun Falls and it is still being run by her there. It is still called Regina's Savannah's Grill. When it was on Bobby Brown it was the place to go. She is still doing well though in Calhoun Falls. She serves a great breakfast and tasty burgers. I spent so much of my childhood at her original grill. I seem to recall my mom working there some, maybe as a second job. My mom has never been too proud to work two or three jobs to provide for us.

It's funny now. Sometimes people will see me at Regina's and ask her if she knows Clay Page. She'll reply, 'Do I know Clay Page? He grew up in our place on Bobby Brown.' At home, I will always be regular old Clay to a lot of people. That is just fine with me. That is the way I want it to be. That old original store is still standing as a reminder.

I have not seen Tyler in a while. He is married with two children. Sadly, I see him the least. Jimmy and Tyler were much wilder than me back in the day. I was wild but they had me beat. They did a few things that I was too scared to do growing up. I did my share of mischief, but I was too afraid of my mama to do some stuff. It's the honest truth when I say I couldn't do anything without her finding out about it. If I made the wrong move, she would know it.

Sometimes I would sit it out at home when I caught wind of what Jimmy and Tyler were planning to do. They have settled down and done well for themselves now. I am so proud of them. They still pick at me all the time asking when Maggie and I are getting married. I love her and she has wonderful grandparents. I think a lot of Red and Margaret Jameson, her grandparents that live in Abbeville. They are great folks and have always been extremely nice to me. They are a very respected family in the community."

I told Clay that my first home as an adult was on Dundas Road in Abbeville, several houses from where Red and Margaret still live. Red taught me in school at Abbeville High. Benji Greeson and I interviewed Coach Jameson when we were writing the book about 100 years of Abbeville Panther football. 'It's All About the A.' Small world, the connections Clay and I share.

Brad Evans is next up. He attended school with Clay and knew of Clay, but they traveled in different circles. He didn't meet Clay until their senior year. He had not gotten into music like Clay. He had begun singing with a group at churches in middle school and high school. He confessed he did not how to play a guitar back then. He realized that he needed people to play the guitar at places he performed and sometimes it was a hassle to find somebody. He decided to learn how to play to solve that problem. In his senior year as he learned to play the guitar, he wrote a few songs. He sent them to Clay telling him he could use them since he did the music and songs. Clay refused to just take the songs from Brad. Instead he insisted that Brad record and sing them. He credits Clay with being the reason he even plays publicly. While Brad had been interested in doing this, he had never envisioned it. Brad is now grateful that Clay pushed him into giving it a try, refusing to take no as an option.

Their relationship began in 2014. The music obviously brought them together and they hit it off. He ended up recording those songs he had tried to give to Clay at his Elberton recording studio. Brad's songs were eventually recorded on the Southbound CD in the Nashville recording studio. Brad wrote 'I'll Be the One' and

'Southbound' for that CD. On the Downhome CD Brad contributed his song 'Buy Back Time.'

Brad currently resides in Athens. He moved to Athens in 2016 and attended Athens Tech there with a plan to transfer to the University of Georgia. He completed his goal at UGA earning a degree in Special Ed. He completed his first year teaching Special Education, but the year had been disrupted by the Covid-19 pandemic making it a unique year. He has no doubt that God led him to this as his calling. Brad expands on his and Clay's relationship.

> "I have always enjoyed playing with Clay. I think we feed off each other. Clay is a serious musician, incredibly talented. I, on the other hand, enjoy getting in a good rib on him. I like for people to see a different side of him. We traveled to California on a trip providing excellent material to be used on stage."

Hold tight. We are about to venture into a segment I will call 'The Greyhound Express, A Bus Whodunit.'

> "We were originally going to take a Megabus from San Jose, California to Los Angeles. We decided against taken the Megabus because we didn't want to wait on it. We instead opted for a Greyhound. I'm not sure if this was the worst mistake we made or the most interesting choice. It wasn't our best choice as it turned out.
>
> The Greyhound was packed and filled with an assortment of interesting characters. At a halfway point the bus stopped at a little gas station in the middle of nowhere. It reminded me of a place you might see on a cartoon with tumbleweeds blowing about in the middle of the desert. The lady bus driver announced on the bus's speaker that we had stopped because someone has peed on the bus. We have two options; either get a new bus or disinfect this one. Everyone was ordered along with their luggage to disembark. There was nowhere to go except inside the little gas station. While we were inside, a storm came up causing the lights to flicker and eventually knocking out the power. Rats were everywhere, running about our feet. Our bus

driver just left all of us there saying another bus would pick us up. Hours and hours passed with no bus arriving. Clay and I were trying to locate an Uber. Cost for an Uber was a hundred bucks but by then we felt it might be worth it. Problem, no Uber would come to our location.

Finally, another Greyhound arrived. It wasn't our promised Greyhound though. This bus driver had no idea that the other driver had stranded a busload of passengers. We all needed a ride to LA so somehow, he managed to fit everyone on his bus. We did eventually arrive in LA in the wee hours of the morning."

Did you identify the pee culprit?

"We had a good idea because she appeared to be up to some new tricks when we loaded onto the new bus. Other passengers nipped her antics in the bud over her pulling stuff by that point. This is one heck of a memorable experience and a story we have gotten plenty of millage telling. I've heard someone say the stuff you are going through seems terrible at the time but can often be the best tales told afterwards. This one was like riding a rollercoaster for a cheap thrill and later sharing the ride with those who never rode one."

This adventure sounded like the perfect song to cowrite.

"To be honest we wondered how we made it out of that one alive, especially after being out in the middle of nowhere like that. We were heading to LA because Clay was playing some shows there. We had stopped by to visit one of his American Idol friends in Santa Cruz, California. He played a few gigs there and then we were headed to LA. We met up with Idol winner, Laine Hardy. He and Clay had become friends. We hung out with Laine for a while. Clay played his scheduled shows and we eventually arrived back to the green grass of Georgia."

Clay was heading to Nashville to cut the Southbound CD when his Papa Ricky Haggerty was basically on his deathbed. You were scheduled to meet Clay in Nashville for the recording session. Tell me about that from your perspective.

> "I believe this was my first time visiting Nashville. Clay had the studio session scheduled to record the songs we had written, and he wanted me to attend. I wasn't sure if the song Southbound was going to make it on the CD. I kind of pushed for him to add it and as it turned out, it ended up being the title of the CD. As I recall, I was on my way to Nashville and Clay texted me saying he was going to stop by and see his granddaddy. He told me he felt it was something he needed to do before heading back to Nashville. It was fine with me. I had access to Clay's place in Nashville.
>
> When he arrived, we did the studio session and recorded the songs. Clay was struggling with what he should do, stay or head back to Greenville to be with him. I encouraged him to return and take care of his granddaddy, then come back to Nashville and finish his business there. I didn't think his granddaddy would want him giving up on his Nashville aspirations. He did go back after we wrapped things up.
>
> The coolest thing for me in the studio was we were surrounded by these professionals who had played on plenty of recordings. We were two kids from Elberton that had doodled these songs on notebook paper and here we were. Adam Shoenfeld was there. Clay and he had become buddies by this point. At the time Adam was Tim McGraw's and Jason Aldean's guitar player and that was cool enough for us. He asked if either of us had a publishing deal. Honestly, I had no idea what a publishing deal was at the time. Once I understood, I took this as a compliment coming from him, thinking our songs must be good enough that we should. That is something I will always remember from the Nashville trip. I thoroughly enjoyed sitting in the studio watching them work on our songs in the recording studio that we had written on notebook paper. Amazing seeing them come to life is this Nashville studio. This was the big time. Things you might

think about and dream about and there we were, getting to do it. I thought that was incredible and cool.

Why didn't you and Clay pursue a publishing deal after Shoenfeld insinuated you should?

"I was never offered one. If someone would have offered, I would have taken them up on it. My ideal scenario now would be teaching and collecting publishing checks from the mailbox. I think Clay just enjoys being in front of people. He is a different guy when he gets on stage. That's why I enjoy ribbing him when we are on stage together to allow the audience to see that guy I saw when we were riding Greyhounds, that he is more drawn to the stage and putting on a show."

Give me some of your ribbing techniques to get under Clay's skin.

"There was this one time when he said we just need to get us a hotel room. I knew what he was talking about. He just wanted us to get a room so that we could writes songs. I said people might think it was kind of funny two dudes getting hotel rooms everywhere. I would say this to him on stage without warning him I was going to do it and it would totally catch him off guard. There are so many stories they run together because I try to pull them as often as possible.

I jab at him with little things because music is his business. I have my teaching. I can do music when I wish as a side gig. I may not take it as seriously as Clay does. This is not a knock on him. It is his life so he should take it seriously. I try to make sure he is having a good time, even if it is at his own expense. If I can get you a little chuckle and loosen him up it is a better show for everybody.

I must be cautious about what stories Clay really wants out there. Back to California, another reason that trip was so crazy was because obviously they have opportunities in LA that are legal that aren't in Georgia. We got into that a little from an experimental standpoint. It made the Greyhound ride interesting sampling some of these and becoming one with the people on the bus. I felt this was their normal routine and I will just leave it at that. I think Clay took a photograph of every rock we passed on the side of the road while riding the Greyhound. I finally told him that I thought he had taken pictures of the same rock and now he had three pictures of it. Clay is all into taking photos for social media. I just regularly go with the flow.

Clay and I have played some interesting places. We have played anywhere from hog trials to plenty of flatbeds and pastures. It was somewhere nearby in Georgia that we played a hog trials event. Competitors had dogs and they would set free a wild hog to see how quickly the dogs could bay the hog. After the competition Clay and I entertained them, playing on a flatbed truck. I think that was our first gig together. I still have the check to commemorate it. That was big for me, my first time being payed to play and sing.

There is no dude that works as hard as Clay with a genuine passion for what he does. I would not be doing it if it weren't for Clay. I wouldn't be playing music; I would be listening to it. Clay and I have always gotten along. At no time have we had a misunderstanding. I understood his goal from the beginning and would never stand in his way. What kind of friend would I be if I stood in the way of him obtaining his dream? I have tried to be there for him anyway I can; promoting him, doing anything I can help.

Clay will focus on his music and you might not hear from him for a while, then, out of blue, he will send me a song and ask me to listen to it. We might not talk for months and then we'll get together as if we had been hanging out yesterday. Clay can be a little scatterbrained. Most anyone will tell you that about him.

I just thought of another funny story. We had just played on a flatbed trailer in North Carolina. Clay had applied sunscreen. After we finished his eyes were very red. He complained about them burning saying he had used the Mickey Mouse sunscreen on his eyes. He thought because it had Mickey Mouse on it, it meant no tears. I told him I didn't think sunscreen is meant to go in your eyes. On that same trip, a guy asked for Clay and me to sign an eight-way cord plug outlet. It was like an outdoor extension cord. He brought it to the stage and asked us to autograph it. That was the strangest autograph I had ever given. We signed his plug under the tent. I was curious if he was going to save it or keep using. I figured he should probably use it because it was losing value if it had my name on it.

Clay is scatterbrained for sure, but at the same time, some of the best times I have had were when we were in his studio in Elberton. Often, we would eat dinner after having been in the studio all day and then we stay there until one or two in the morning. This was cool to me because I was just getting into playing music. This was a bonding experience for us. The first time we met we kind of hit it off. I have always respected Clay for grinding and pursing his music career. From where we come from people don't expect you to make it. They see you as a guy sitting on a stool and playing. Clay never cared what those people said or thought; he just did it anyway. I think there is something to be said for that. He had a good thing going at his Elberton studio before heading off to Nashville. He felt it was his time to go and give it a try.

Clay would not be where he is without Maggie Jameson. She can run the show 100%. Clay can get up there and sing and she can do the rest. She can handle tickets, setting up shows at venues. I have fortunately never made it on Maggie's bad side. I pray for those who ever do. I can tell by her demeanor and by what she has told me that she is a no BS kind of gal. You don't teach high school like she does without being that way. She takes no prisoners. It is a little different for me, teaching Special Education, but I do coach baseball and deal with the general public. You can't let them think they have something on you.

Have you and Clay collaborated recently on any music projects?

"We planned to rent us a cabin and hang out and write but then the Covid came along and derailed that. It has always been easy for Clay and me to meet over Facetime to talk about songs we have written. 'I'll Be the One' and 'Southbound' were written while I was in Athens and Clay in Nashville. "Buy Back Time' was written in his apartment in Nashville and, when he got to the studio, he felt it needed a little extra, so he Facetimed me from a Nashville Chick-fil-A. We finished the song then. We actually got to do that one with Adam Shoenfeld on the Southbound CD."

If you could give Clay any advice about his career or life what would you tell him?

"I think I've told Clay my opinion numerous times. For the most part he is going to do things his way. I have told him there are plenty of people in the world but there is only one you. Love the fact that you are who you are. What you see is what you get. He is a lot more country than you hear on the radio and that isn't a bad thing. Be who you are. He has always bet on himself. That is a good thing for anyone to do."

Do you have any thoughts about where his direction should be, writing and publishing music or performing?

"There are plenty of folks like Luke Bryan, that started out by writing songs and now look where he is now. Many write and publish to get their foot in the door. Given the right opportunity I don't know why Clay wouldn't allow someone to record one of his songs. He has fished a few out there but didn't get any well served bites. I think he enjoys performing and desires making it this way instead of writing and publishing. I can not fault him for doing it the way he wants to do it if that is what makes him happy. Clay has never taken the easy way. It might be easier to make it the publishing route but if he makes it straight out being himself, he can tell everyone he bet on himself and made it. That is a better story to tell."

Had you been performing anywhere before this pandemic happened?

"I had put it on the backburner this year focusing on my first year of teaching. I had thought when summer rolled around, I would play in the bars. I have a main check coming in so I can play the songs I want when I do perform. I was looking forward to this before Covid halted it. I am excited I will be doing the show in Abbeville with Benji Greeson, Square on the Air June 14th to kick things off. It is a lot more professional than something I should be performing on. I'm praying we are getting close to being out of this mess we have been in."

Has Athens treated the pandemic seriously?

"I think so, but now we have had those protests about the recent tragedy. I think Athens took it more seriously than Elberton. I think they thought they were so small it wouldn't impact them, but I believe it is hitting them now. I just returned from North Carolina. I was the best man at a wedding. We had a bachelor party in the middle of riots. That was a bit of a bummer, but we managed the best we could.

Any last Clay thoughts, Brad?

Clay has written a song titled after the book, 'Somewhere In Between'. I think it might be one of his best songs and did not help him write it. He played it when he appeared on the first Square episode with Benji. I told him when this Covid was over it would be the perfect time to put out that song because with the pandemic everyone has been finding themselves 'somewhere in between'."

Brad Evans shared a few of his favorite photographs.

Brad and Clay at Elberton Elks Lodge

**Brad and Clay Sold Out
at Athens Mellow Mushroom**

Clay and Brad Performing on a Flatbed Trailer at the Hog Trials

In Nashville Studio Recording Southbound

Brad, Clay, and David Dorn in Nashville Recording Studio

Clay Just 'Plane' Tired

Something

Clay began our conversation in this segment thinking back weeks ago on his trip to Charlotte, N.C. That drive filled with personal reflections and self assessments still haunted him. What had been somewhat of a crossroad in his life, an intersection of where he was, where he wanted to go, and where he had ended up, had certainly sent him down a road he had not been prepared to travel. That right turn had opened his eyes and had lit a fire, the flames being fueled by a new reckoning and purpose. One can never forget one's roots and what is most important in the journey.

> "That event struck a nerve. I realized that I should be willing to give more, maybe something I have not done enough of because I have been so busy focusing on my career. I lost focus of what means the most, being more charitable than I have been in the past. I had put it on the backburner, having even turned down some charity work, allowing myself to be too consumed by my career and my goals.
>
> It just hit me. I haven't been giving back nearly enough this year and I have been blessed to be where I am. The last couple of weeks I have shifted my primary focus and have been doing some charity events, still in the self assessing and learning curve. December, my agenda has been to give back as much as possible. Maybe I cannot give as much financially as I would want but I'm giving my time, something directly from my heart.

Clay made an unannounced visit to the Fayetteville, N.C. VA Health Care Center before heading over to the Fayetteville VA Medical Center where he played a few songs for the community center residents. He then visited an orphanage near Dunn, N.C. He followed this up the next day by attending the South Hart Elementary School in Hartwell, Georgia where he read 'Santa is Coming to Georgia' to a classroom of students as they sat in front of a fire displayed on the classroom television. The next night he would be venturing to Eatonton, Georgia before appearing in Monteagle, Tennessee at Jesse's Grill the next night where he would be encouraging those attending to bring a toy. Clay would be participating in a toy drive at Elberton Elks Lodge to continue his December tour of giving back.

"I'm excited to be heading down to Eatonton, Georgia, but a bit concerned with the frigid weather and nasty rain. It wouldn't surprise me if there was a freezing rain and sleet mixture. I cleaned up my Isuzu Rodeo for the first time in quite a while, super proud of that. I have been putting more miles on it, traveling to Fayetteville then back to Georgia. I will then be traveling to Tennessee. That is a lot of miles in just a few days. I was a little nervous, but I checked the oil and the water. She is still running.

I traveled to Nashville a few weeks ago also and ended up declining a management contract. This has been dogging me for a while. Should I, or shouldn't I? My gut has been troubling me about taking that next step. It's tough giving up some of the ownership over to another after having built it myself over the pass eleven years. Possibly a swaying factor in this had to be my family and what they thought as well. My grandma Camilla, Maggie and other family members agreed that I needed to seek a second opinion before I decided.

I did seek the advice of a lawyer while in Nashville. His exact words to me were, 'I can get you out of a divorce in two years but getting out of a management contract might take five or six years.' Basically, he advised me to weigh my options carefully before deciding. That was the perfect eyeopener to assist me in making a serious decision in my career. Maybe I'm just not quite ready yet. That lifted one burden off my shoulders. Coming to terms with this even though it was tough. I realize that at some point I am going to have to take that next step. Now just doesn't feel like that time. Once that was off my back, the last few weeks have been fantastic, the juices flowing. I've assumed managerial control with new vigor, taking charge, making contacts, and booking tons of appearances."

Focus was redirected toward Clay's music. What inspires Clay Page to write songs? Let's explore the method behind the magic of songwriting, the meaning behind his songs and even those who have impacted the direction of his music.

> "When it comes to writing music, I must be inspired by an event in my life or a specific mood I might be in. This is something I had been missing while living in Nashville. I was forcing myself to write more but I was missing the point. Writing instead of living it. The full inspirational part of it was a missing component."

Take the readers through some of your more memorable songs and what inspired them.

> "One of the most memorable writing sessions for me had to be with someone I consider a friend, Will Bundy. We met while I was working at the gym in Nashville. We talked about hooking up and doing a song sometime. That's Nashville lingo for writing a song. Will and I did eventually hook up. He brought a young lady named Lydia Vaughn with him. We sat down and wrote a song called 'Roots and Wings'. It was about leaving home and chasing a dream.
>
> Will and I both had family illnesses going on at the time which amplified the feelings within the lyrics. The three of us were sharing similar emotions. The experience was almost therapeutic. I believe, even today, it has been one of the biggest songs that I have ever been a part of. Many told us that it could be a career changing song. Will has done a demo of it. I had to leave the session before we completed it, but Will and Leida finished it. While I contributed, the two of them drove the bus on the song. I really wanted to sing it on American Idol, but publishing legalities prevented me from doing so. Sadly, Will and I have not kept in touch since my Idol experience. I would love to see that song land someplace with someone recording it or me doing it if no one else is interested. It would be a shame to see it just setting on the shelf.
>
> 'Something' is the song I released as a single. This one was incredibly special to me. I don't often listen to my own

music, but this song has helped me through some tough times in my life. Rob Snider and I wrote this song. It evolved by me telling Rob my story of being from Elberton, concerns about my Uncle Norman's failing health, and other things impacting my life at the time. He suggested we put it to music. It is my most streamed song with over 11,000 streams on Spotify. I am thinking about making a music video out of it. I am often inspired when listening to the lyrics when which make for better days."

Clay shares a few lines from 'Something.'

Amy is a looker and she's waiting dirty tables
In Savannah way out on the coast
They say she's crazy raising three little babies
All on her own.

"The core of that song is we all have something bringing us down this side of the clouds. It's tough to recall the lyrics without my guitar in my hands."

I advised Clay not to take up his guitar while he was driving and talking to me on the phone. They do not make hands free guitars just yet. That might be more dangerous than texting. He laughed and then continued.

"This song has been really special, rating up there with 'Roots and Wings', 'Something' and another one I have written, 'Lonely Highway to Georgia.' I wrote it while traveling alone down the interstate one night. I was really stuck in traffic. If you listen, everything in that song, every word, was what was on my mind, and where I was during the time. So many of my songs have been special to me."

Who most inspired you to begin writing music?

"Oh man, that's a really good question. I have not actually thought about who inspired me to write my own music. Some artists have surely been inspirational. *Urban Cowboy*, the movie probably had some impact. George Strait influenced me with his character, Dusty, in the movie, *Pure Country*. That was when I was in my George Strait time in high school, wearing the wrangler jeans and cowboy hat, singing but I didn't have my own songs. Plenty of artists have inspired me; heavy hitters like Hank Williams, Sr., Merle Haggard, Waylon Jennings and Lynyrd Skynyrd. I was always drawn to the old timers, throwbacks to country music. I went through an Allman Brothers stage. Lukas Nelson most recently has been one. He is a phenomenal artist and guitar player. His lyrics are everything.

I have always listened to all types of music. Even rap. Some rap music has inspired me, believe it or not. It can often be very vulgar though. I am not a fan of that but there is a lot of truth behind some of the rap lyrics. One thing about rap music, I have always been envious of how they can say real things and make it sound cool. If a country artist would say some of these things, people would be saying, 'What?'

What's your take on Kanye West's transformation to Christian music?

"I think it is great if he's found the Lord. I believe that should be all our attitudes. Nobody knows your relationship with God other than you. I applaud him.

It might be a shock to some that I listen to rap music a lot while I am in the gym exercising. When I am driving down the road at 2 AM in the morning I often listen to a Podcast called the Breakfast Club which is nothing more than hip hop interviews with artists. It's weird how I can sometimes relate more to that culture and genre than my own."

I told Clay, from my perspective it was quite interesting that he was pursing a country music career, yet he was totally into the rap and hip-hop genres; not that there is anything wrong with it other than being interesting.

"I guess it begins with my roots, starting from a humble beginning on the bottom and working my way through it to

> get where I am now. I can relate to that journey and quest to be in a better place. It is about turning our lives from nothing into something. There are plenty of rap artists that may inspire me from a career standpoint. They may not inspire me musically. Instead they inspire me as a person basically from relating to where they began and what they have made of themselves."

I had to toss this in, thinking back to Clay talking about having the loudest truck in Elberton. I asked did he have one of those teeth chattering sound systems as well. He admitted that he had been known to crank up the volume, confirming again that he was a punk in high school. He professed that he minded his own business but could be quite noticeable on the streets of Elberton. Yep, he could have been one of those behind me rattling my windows and teeth. He said, yep, he could have been guilty as charged between no mufflers and the music. Thinking back on those days triggered another thought from Clay.

> "I ventured over to Abbeville when they were in the semi final game before the state championship last year. I felt for them when they lost their bid for a possible fifth state title in a row. I am not into football, but I felt that loss along with them. The entire stadium was quiet when the last second ticked off the clock."

Obviously, I can relate to this. Benji Greeson and I have cowritten two books about Abbeville, S.C. Panther Football covering 102 years of small-town tradition. Author privilege and shameless plug, the books, 'All About the A' and 'All About the Angels in the Backfield, Dawn of a Dynasty'. And a shout out to Clay's Maggie who coaches the Panther cheerleaders, the main reason Clay had attended the game.

> "I've had a lot of artists who have inspired me from all genres. My philosophy has always been, no matter what genre you are in, own it. I sometimes have issues with the infusions of different genres in music. While most can be great, others are trash to me. I say whatever you choose, own it and do it to your full potential. Some might consider my music trash, but I give it my all, dedicating 100%.

When you can feel the song being sung versus just listening to a song, is what makes it real to me. That is what resonates with me and what I enjoy the most out of music."

Do you have anyone from a local perspective that influenced your music and inspired you?

"Obviously, my parent's music collection. I must credit the Broad River Band with friend Jimmy Jones' dad, David, as being a positive influence on me. Corey Smith was an inspiration, a local boy who went big. Brantley Gilbert another northeastern Georgian impacted my thinking about music. My guitar teacher Vernon Brown in Calhoun Falls, and my Uncle Norman were instrumental in my life. Jeff Ledbetter is a guitar player that did as much as anyone for the direction I have taken. He's a phenomenal picker and person."

What was the first song that you wrote?

"That would be 'Pure Country', my very first. The first song I ever learned to play was 'Hey Good Looking' by Hank Williams, Sr. I still enjoy playing that song. My dad turned me on to the Texas country music. The Texas country music scene is totally different from the southeast scene."

Are you a Bob Wills fan, the Texas swing music?

"I'd be lying if I said I knew any of his music. I do remember Waylon Jennings having that song, 'Bob Wills is Still the King'. I feel my music is more the Bakersfield, California, Merle Haggard sound, and more toward the Texas music than southeastern. I tell people my music is more new old school. There is a scene out in Texas called the Red Dirt. It is more of a throwback to 90's country music. It thrives, and guys make a comfortable living singing and doing their own thing without traveling to Nashville. They make their living just playing in Texas. It is a very tightknit group when it comes to that music scene.

I have been to Texas quite a few times. I have been listening to this scene since I was sixteen. My goal had always been to go to Texas and play music out there. In this past year I have lived that dream, going there, and playing some. It is an amazing concept. The radio stations support and promote local music. We have a scene as well in the southeast, but Nashville has the monopoly on country music from this region. That is why I went to Nashville in the first place.

There are a ton of local artists on around my neck of the woods who are great talents, but they are not being promoted or showcased like they are in Texas. The local venues are more utilized as background music establishments instead of having a setup more suitable to showcase the artists like in Texas. It is terrible that customers going to these venues automatically perceive the musicians playing them as purely background setups located in the corner. Texas takes a lot of pride in the music and those performing. The venues are set with stages and phenomenal sound systems, realizing the customers are there to listen to great music. They sell tickets to events instead of offering base pay for the artist performing in them. Buying tickets to performances equates to your being invested in the event and more likely to be engaged in it."

Have you established any connections with the Texas scene?

"I have. Jade Flores is a Texas girl who competed on Idol with me. She is a phenomenal singer. She has introduced me to a lot of folks out there. Jade and her family are wonderful people. I had a run this past summer in Texas, one of the craziest runs I have ever had in my life. This one time I had been up about 24 hours straight when we arrived in Texas. After the plane trip I drove to a place in Texas and played. I literally got out of the rental car and walked on stage.

Jade and I played several more shows afterward. There was some sort of mix up in the schedule for one of the shows and they were not expecting us that day. Jade's mom was having none of that and found another gig for us. That is how great Jade, and her family are. Darren Eubanks, another Idol contestant was there as well last summer. We had an American Idol reunion, performing in Texas at the Firehouse Castro Park.

Kevin Mitchell is another. He has been playing guitar with me. He is from the Dallas-Fort Worth area. It is funny how he and I met. I was coming out of a bar in Nashville and he introduced himself to me as a guitar player from the DFW. I told him, 'Dude, no way.' I have enjoyed that scene forever. Kevin and his family have welcomed me with open arms anytime I am in the area. Kevin's dad, Patrick, is a world renown chef." (Note: Patrick is an Executive Chef/Culinary Advisor for Ben E. Keith Foods based in Ft. Worth, Texas. "He has won over 40 national and international awards, including a gold medal in the Culinary World Cup in Luxembourg, 2014.) It has been amazing getting to know Kevin's family. Kevin still lives in Nashville and offers me a place to crash when I go back.

What are some of the memorable songs that you have written?

"One was 'When We Were Kids'. That one was about me, Jimmy Jones, and Tyler McKellar. It is a descriptive song that people who knew me would know the characters without me naming them. It is an incredibly special song, so real to me. The lyrics are about us having skater shoes on our feet, that time when we were going through the skateboard phase. It goes on saying how my mama dropped us off at Fallen Creek, which is the elementary school we attended. It talks about how we thought we were cool. In the second verse it talks about how high school was fun as hell, how we made our teachers yell.

We did not mean anything by the stuff we were doing. We were just trying to make a scene and be noticed. This song probably summarized my childhood if anything did. At the end of the song it states that we are grown men, one buddy in the United States Marines, another starting a family, and I still had not put my guitar down. Thinking about it now, I should consider re-recording it, a fresh recording. It would go hand and hand with this book and my story."

Clay reflects on his process of song writing.

"Before I moved to Nashville, I didn't have an urge to do any cowriting. I just figured I could write my own. After moving there though and writing with others I have learned that it is good to have cowriters. Besides booking shows and performing, I have a desire to return to Nashville in 2020 and rekindle the songwriting. I have a full week booked in February to focus on writing sessions. Doing this biography has opened my eyes to so many things. I cannot thank you enough, Tom, for taking the time to do this and how talking with you has elevated my self awareness and priorities. I have found a way to refocus my goals and my dreams to accomplish what I had originally set out to do in my career."

Clay, indeed, has discovered himself through this process. He had an urge to talk about the tiny house he lives in on his late Uncle Norman's property.

"I haven't talked much about my tiny house. Last month (November) my focus was on preparing for the release of my new CD and marketing my music while dealing with the management offerings. While in the middle of all this, my granddaddy, James Robinson, was working on my tiny house. We have been updating the ductwork among other projects. Bless my granddaddy because there would be times when I was working on music related stuff and he would be there busting his back. It would make me feel so bad that I was involved in my music while he was there helping me. I spent my fair share of time apologizing to him telling him how I appreciated everything he was doing. Uncle Norman and he are brothers.

The projects are done thanks to him. With 2020 approaching I am on fire, booking shows, and doing charity performances. I imagine I have gotten on too many peoples' nerves with my aggressiveness over the past few weeks. No pun intended, but a new page is about to be turned in this new year ahead. Maggie has been so supportive through the process and putting up with me. I'm focused and trying to make the most of every day."

Sometimes, life tosses eyeopeners your way and when it does it is best you take them to heart and optimize the lesson learned. Clay has had one of those moments while undergoing the process of doing his biography. Pondering and reflecting sometimes happens for a reason. The good Lord does not hand you any more than you can handle, according to scripture says Clay. He looks back at Idol now thinking that maybe he didn't get as much television exposure as he had thought he should have, but maybe the Lord knew something that he didn't. Maybe he had not been as fully prepared for the Idol experience as he should have been, but no denying it, the experience had changed his life.

In this business anxiety is a big part of the grind, but Clay has managed to channel his into being blessed to be able to play music for a living. He adds that it is easy to take it for granted but he is extremely blessed just the same. There are good and bad things in every business, but Clay feels in his heart the good has far outweighed the bad. He has realized that smaller markets are just as important as those in the big cities. Collecting the data is a critical component no matter where or how you perform. His take, it will all work out eventually.

Clay again mentioned his Rodeo with nearly 300,000 road miles on it, thinking back to his other grandfather who bought it for him. While Papa Ricky is no longer with him, he has the vehicle as a wonderful memory and testament to a man he dearly loved. Family means everything to Clay. That is why he treasures the Rodeo, his tiny house on his Uncle Norman's property, and the love, support, and devotion his granddaddy Robinson offers him.

Clay laughs about his road warrior Isuzu, thinking to something he once read about musicians.

> *Musicians are the only people I know who will travel 500 miles for $100 with $1500 of equipment in the back of a $300 car.*

Testament to that thought, Clay was heading from Elberton Georgia to Eatonton, Georgia for an appearance and would leave the next morning for a location near Chattanooga, Tennessee, after having traveled to North Carolina days prior. While playing music is a gifted and privileged experience according to him, it comes with a cost, the constant traveler doing what it takes to keep the dream alive. Nobody promised that following one's dream would be a cakewalk. It is anything but. Ask any musician. They have followed this weary and long path if they were serious about their worth as Clay likes to call it. Clay explains his current run.

> "Ideally, I would prefer to be playing with a band right now and at venues where all I have to do is show up, walk in, and do a soundcheck and then hang out. But tis the season to do what needs to be done."

Without an agent or manager Clay controls his own destiny. He performs the responsibilities of being the booking agent, contacting venues, negotiating the price for an appearance, and promoting as best he can. He utilizes his website to post a list of upcoming appearances and any perks for attending. His Rodeo is his one-man bus per se for hauling him and any necessary equipment to the venues on his schedule. Clay does not complain or grumble about it. He just gets it done and commits totally to what he signs up to do. This is not the first rodeo in his career, over a decade of pursuing a dream, one that can be elusive at times, but forever within his grasp. Sometimes you just do what you must do to keep it real.

A thought popped into my head during the interview and I ran this up the flagpole to Clay. Had he ever considered asking Vernon Brown to play with him at a local gig or even record with him on a song. It seemed to me to be the perfect tribute and exclamation point to his blossoming career. Vernon, eighty-eight and still healthy and playing would be the perfect complement from my perspective.

> "Man, I have not. That would be cool. I am doing a lot of local appearances right now, one being the Elberton Elk Lodge. I owe them my deepest gratitude. They created a

fund while I was competing on Idol to help offset some of my traveling expenses. Nothing beats my hometown for their unconditional support. It is unreal what a small town will do for you. That is why I love small towns so much. While the big cities are great with all the traveling I have been doing, there is always something missing when I'm in the larger cities. Small towns offer that support you cannot find elsewhere. When in need, people will literally offer you the shirt off their backs. The smaller towns are where I feel the strong fan base. People are real, appreciative, and sincere. It brings me back to my roots.

Too often, it is easy to have your eyes set on the bigger picture and forget what got you there in the first place. There is something to be said about opportunities to travel to California, compete in Hollywood, going to Texas, and enjoying it fully, but at the end of the day I am from Elberton, Georgia. I will always be from Elberton, Georgia and I always be no matter where life takes me. Everything comes back to Elberton, Georgia. Too often as careers explode the artists tend to forget about their humble beginnings and who was responsible for them being where they are now. Striving for a balance isn't necessarily easy.

I think sometimes people perceive me as an ass when I blow them off, saying I cannot play certain events or certain dates. I am not trying to be an ass, but instead I'm trying to be a smart businessman. I am after all, Clay Page's agent as well. It's a constant struggle to take care of business and keep my feet on the ground. I try my best to not come across as jerk. I'm really focusing much of my time and energy during the holiday season giving back to my community and charities in the area. At the Elk Lodge we will be doing a toy drive for the Salvation Army in town.

Maggie, being a teacher, just recently shared a story with me about orphans in the area at Greenwood, South Carolina's Connie Maxwell Children's Home. One little girl had a wish for Christmas. All she wanted was a pack of ink pens. Someone had bought her some pens and it lit her

> up, bringing tears to her eyes getting something as simple as that. This is what it is all about. It is so easy to forget what pushes some of us and what's important in our lives until you see or experience something like this. When it happens, it kicks you in your seat and sits you down. It makes you realize just how much you must be thankful for. If you give unconditionally you will be rewarded tenfold. I am trying my best, especially this time of the year, to give more. I have rested so much better, at peace, knowing I have pushed myself hard in December, and I have done my best to give back."

Have you ever considered writing and recording a Christmas song? Most accomplished artists seem to gravitate to this premise sooner or later.

> "I was asked to do a remembrance service in Abbeville a few weeks ago at Harris Funeral Home. The only Christmas music I have done is Robert Earl Keen's 'Merry Christmas from the Family'. I have not done any other Christmas or Gospel music. I have never written one but that is something I should consider. I'd have to get into that realm to do it though."

Clay continues to relate to the transition he has found himself in lately.

> "There are times when I am so busy doing my music and everything that supports it, I'm feeling incredibly great. What is easy to lose scope of is too often it impacts the valuable family time, especially during the Christmas season. Sometimes I can allow Maggie and me time to be pushed to the backburner, not intentionally, but it does happen. It's always a constant battle to find that perfect balance. Family is important and is a priority, even if sometimes it doesn't appear that way to the ones that I love."

Are you currently writing any new songs?

"I have a folder on my computer labeled 2019 ideas. I bet I have ten to thirteen melodies and guitar riffs. My process of writing must be by inspiration or a special event in my life. I think I just made this word up, but I sometimes must be inspired 'guitarsly'. I must be inspired guitar wise. This has to do with me originally having started out as just a guitar player. That is why Lukas Nelson's stuff inspires me. He is a lyricist and a musician who can play guitar and write music. It is so real.

There are several artists, in my humble opinion, that are just artist. They have the looks and can sing. They may sport a guitar, but they are up there just strumming. On the flipside, you have those who can really play an instrument and can also sing. If you can play an instrument and can project your message to your audience, the singing is just one more element.

Summarizing my 2019. I have been blessed. Sometimes the Lord puts just enough on your plate that He thinks you can handle. He certainly did this for me. This year has been a defining time in my career. I can only imagine what 2020 has in store."

At the time of this segment Clay could have never envisioned the roadblocks 2020 would toss his way. A pandemic storm would wreak havoc on his plans.

Same Old Song, New Beginnings

It is 2020. Clay has reassessed his life over the past year. The Idol experience has been a life changer. Undaunted though, he lays out his plans for the new year ahead, one for sure to have more challenges and hopefully more breakthroughs in his young career. He is excited about the start thus far and it is still only January.

> "This business is much like that of a person who does landscaping as their job. This week may be great then you go through a period without being paid because there is are no lawns to mow or other chores to hold you over. It can often be feast or famine for musicians as well. I am still at the do or die situation. I can play every weekend somewhere, money to live on, but this, as I have said many times, is not helping the big picture and my long-term aspirations. I must be extremely cautious when taking this approach, so that I do not saturate the areas where I am doing well. It is a tough balance, but it has forced me to seek new markets.
>
> The nature of the beast changes quickly when you are attempting to emerge into new markets, uncharted territory so to speak. You are often subjected to taking what you can get. It might not necessarily be what ideally what you want. This has prompted me to do my research. I have used the data from my Facebook account to home in on the cities where people are listening to my music. I have a texting method that I have been utilizing as well to determine where my audiences might be.
>
> Then, there is the old fashion technique. Just get on the phone and make connections with venues, inquiring as to whether they do live music. If the contacts are interested, I forward them an email with a list of my music. This is not the easiest to do. It can often be stressful, but I am my manager and booking agent, so it goes with the territory. While I have been doing this over ten years there are plenty of places that do not know me nor my music.

A new year is a time for making resolutions for most people. I have instead established my 2020 goal list. One of my goals is to hit at least three experimental markets. These markets to me are locations like California, Australia, and Canada. These can be places that I have never played, or the numbers are low in them. I was pleasantly shocked at the number of people listening to my music in Australia. My prayers go out to Australia with the fires they are dealing with now. It is on my to do list to travel 'down under.' I have Canadian listeners as well. I will be in Santa Cruz, California in February. My third or fourth trip there. Santa Cruz is one of my favorites, one of the coolest places I have ever been.

I am heading to Nashville again in February. Several places are already booked. I will be promoting my new CD this time. I also have a single that I plan to release in May titled 'Checked Out'. It is about growing up, a summertime song I have written with Alex Dooley. I plan to shoot a music video on the lake as well. I'm going to be recording a video for the song 'Something' the end of January.

I am not sure I will be back in the recording studio in 2020 with everything else I have going on. My focus for this year will be playing the shows and knocking down some debt. It is an easy trap to fall into in this business, spending more than you're taking in. It's a tough balance, doing these things and having the time to write songs."

Clay, while looking forward, reflects on 2019. He had those regrets about picking on the kid during his biking days in Calhoun Falls. Remember, thinking about it, he reached out to the man via a message. That relationship has since progressed. He has talked with him a couple of times face to face, now appreciative of the little kid he had once picked on now being a person who has served this country militarily. Good things come from these heartfelt situations, making peace long overdue. His grandma Camilla had asked him to go to the VA in Anderson, S.C. recently to visit a family member and play some music for him. Clay showed up and played for him inside his room there.

> "After I was done, I left the room and outside in the hallway there was an elderly gentleman in a wheelchair, a WWII veteran. His mind was sharp, and he began telling me stories of his war times. This was quite inspirational. It made me realize that I need to do this more often; give back to those who served our country.
>
> In the month of December, I completed a tour down home where we earned several thousand dollars of contributions and toys. This consisted of a couple of VA visits in Fayetteville, North Carolina and at a VA in Charleston, S.C. I also played at an orphanage while in North Carolina and met a couple of children interested in music. I did a toy drive at the Elberton Elks Club as well; bring a toy to the show. This was my time to give back. Something wonderful that I experienced for the first-time during December. I am blessed and must and must never forget that.
>
> I can't say this enough. My December this year was different than any I have ever had. I had been so busy last year that it honestly felt great to give back for a change. I read a Christmas story to a kindergarten class in Hartwell, Georgia. Kids at that age are so honest. I really enjoyed my time spent with them. Maybe this is the beginning of a new tradition."

I told Clay that I envisioned a song writing opportunity given the subject he had just covered, Christmas, veterans, and children. I suggested he add this to his 2020 goals. Clay regrets that ten years ago he did not have the mindset he has now. He added how truly blessed he is.

Clay continues,

> "When I head to Nashville in February, I plan to hook up with a few old friends like Adam Shoenfeld who basically produced my last CD. I have plans to do some writing with him while there. Baker Grissom, a buddy of mine, has a cut on my last two projects as a songwriter-cowriter on at least two songs. Hope to see him as well. I am playing the

NWTF banquet. To those not familiar with the acronym, it is the National Wild Turkey Federation. It is being held at the Gaylord Opryland Resort and Convention Center in Nashville.

Speaking of wild turkeys, I have missed doing some of the things I love like hunting and fishing. On my list is to return to my roots as often as I can this year. This past year I have focused on my music and working, promoting, and have gotten away from the simple joys in life. I mentioned to Maggie that this might do me some good, clearing the head and all. It might shock some folks to see me back in the woods or out on the lake. It has been a while for sure. Hunting and fishing are a huge part of country music as well. It defines who I am, who I have always been. I am just an old country boy in mind and heart.

Do people recognize you as a celebrity or as plain Clay Page when they see you out and about in public, especially around Elberton?

"For the most part if I keep my ballcap on I'm good. Sometimes even then there are those that will recognize me. All are usually very respectful in the encounters. When someone walks up to me and asks, are you Clay Page, it throws me off. Often, I am asked for an autograph or a photo with them. This takes me off guard, especially on the home turf. I'm not sure if they are yanking my chain or being serious.

One incident really caught me off guard. It happened while I was in Athens, Georgia one day at Lowes. It was early on a Monday or Tuesday morning and there were not many people in the store at the time. I was totally focused on projects I was working on at home and items I needed to pick up when a guy walked up and took me by surprise. It was tough for me to switch from that mode into Clay the performer mode. I had not expected that encounter.

I spent quite some time with that gentlemen who ended up being a super cool guy. He had been following my music for a long time. I am not always good in these situations. I

> never want to be perceived as ingenuine. I cannot help it. I have always struggled with the interactions, especially when caught by surprise. I try to pull myself together as quickly as possible. Sometimes it works. I was always an introvert and still am in some ways if that makes any sense."

I offered Clay a little friendly advice. Stay true to who you are, and the genuineness will show through loud and clear. Easier said that done, I'm sure. Being yourself is the best road traveled though.

> "It's different when I'm entertaining at a venue. I expect it. I'm in that element and that mode. I don't recall ever being unapproachable or rude to anyone. Some might see it differently, but I try to always remain sincere and appreciative. It's that introverted thing, always a battle. That creates anxiety for me in social situations. For instance, recently I was sick as a dog and dreaded going anywhere in Elberton. I was so sick I did not feel comfortable shaking anyone's hand and spreading germs. I think I may have had Covid. I did not want anyone to think I was being standoffish for my actions. First impressions are important. It was tough for me to even talk. Maggie was out of town, so that left me with few choices, but my mama came through for me, picking up items I needed."

Clay had a show coming up in Abbeville in February and I asked what his expectations for that event were. He talked about how he really loved the town of Abbeville, his birthplace as well as mine. Of course, he was hoping for a sellout at the Abbeville Opera House. I told him I hoped to travel to my hometown from Myrtle Beach for his performance. Sometimes best intentions work. Other times they don't.

Clay continues,

> "So far all is good. My Granddaddy James lives across the road from me. This road where we live used to be my granddaddy's farm before they built the dam, and Lake Russel backwater took it over. We traced back to his great grandfather, that low and behold, lived in Abbeville. And

we discovered his grandmother was from Anderson, S.C. This makes perfect sense for me to love Abbeville even though I grew up in Elberton. It is literally in my blood. I have thoroughly enjoyed delving into my roots."

Wilmington is just a hop and skip from me at the beach. I asked Clay if he had ever considered playing any Myrtle Beach venues.

"I have. I have contacted the Wild Wing Café in several locations including Charleston. I did send an email to a venue in Conway, S.C. that is close to Myrtle Beach. I must be careful when choosing tourist areas though. Many places ask for the maximum performance for the minimum pay. That is tough to do with travel expenses, food, and accommodations not included. That is why they often utilize local bands instead. Same goes for me when I play locally. Places like the beach do remain on my list of possible markets though. I always keep my options open."

I asked Clay if he ever considered trying out for venues like the Carolina Opry or Alabama Theater at the beach. This would offer more of a fulltime employment option performing at these theaters year-round as a member of their regular cast. It is not unusual for them to add entertainers that have had previous success on shows like Idol or America's Got Talent.

"That's not really someplace I envision being right now. Don't take me wrong. I think it is a beautiful thing for someone seeking it. Some performers I met during Idol have taken this route. They have embraced opportunities like this. I think as a musician this would be something cool to do, possibly as a guitar player. I'm not sure this would be best for me in my pursuit to be a singer-songwriter though. I have the utmost respect for anyone who would choose this path if that's what they wish to do. It's awesome to watch them performing on stage in choreographed singing and dancing routines."

Mother Knows Best

I had the most wonderful conversation with Clay's mother, Jennifer. Where better to understand the artist and songwriter than stroll down memory lane with the one responsible for bringing him into this world. A mother's love and honesty never shine through more powerfully and sincerely as from the lips of one who truly cherishes her son. I told Jennifer that I appreciated that Clay had convinced her to chat with me. She laughed, saying he had not really asked but he had instead told her someone was calling that she needed to talk to about him. Clay lives just across the road from his mom in his tiny house that he shares with his beloved Maggie Jameson. Jennifer is in her second marriage. She was born in Anderson, S.C. but grew up in Elberton, Ga. She lived in Abbeville briefly after giving birth to Clay. Papa James Robinson is her paternal father. Clay had certainly shared stories about his Grandfather James.

Jennifer begins,

> "Clay has had plenty of help from my dad and my stepdad, Ricky. My stepdad has passed now but he really helped Clay in his music. My daddy has helped other ways, a man who can build anything and fix anything. My stepdad was more the if you need it, I'll see that you get it, supporter."

Papa Ricky had been instrumental in instilling a strong work ethic in Clay, the man who had done odd jobs to stay busy including power washing.

Grandmother Camilla and Papa Ricky with Clay

"I was a single mom. There were several men that helped me with Clay. My dad was one of these men. My stepdad also filled that void. My Uncle Norman was another key person in his life. A family friend, Tubby Worley also stepped up to influence him. Tubby has really put a lot of time in with Clay over the years. Anytime I was having trouble with Clay, I called Tubby to help."

I shared with Jennifer that Clay told me that he had a tough time pulling anything over on her; she had this knack for sensing when he was up to something.

Jennifer laughed,

> "Oh yes. You could look at Clay and would know if he was up to something. He could not get away with much. All I had to do was look at him and ask a few questions. He would spill it. It might have taken a day or two, but he would break down and tell me."

Let's back pedal and start where life began for young Clay Page.

> "Clay was born in what is now the old Abbeville Memorial Hospital that had been located off Hwy 72. My other two kids say Clay is the golden child. Clay has a brother and sister, Connor, and Gracie. Clay claims they are the golden children. He says that I baby them. Common practice among siblings, each thinking the other takes preference.
>
> I was only seventeen when he was born. I had to grow up very quickly. I attended Calhoun Falls High School up until the day he was born. He ended up being extremely sick when he was about four months old and almost died. He spent 14 days in the hospital. Clay had been diagnosed with Group B Streptococcus. The doctor informed me that we had been truly fortunate that we hadn't found him cold one morning when we woke up. With Group B Strep, most babies die within the first few hours of birth. I guess because of this scary beginning I do tend to lean toward him more."

Where did Clay's name originate? Was he named after anyone in particular?

> "His first name is Michael. The name Michael originated from my brother who was killed in a car wreck. Michael Clayton Page is his full name. I did not want him to be called Michael though because it was my brother's name. When he was born, there was a newspaper article in the Anderson Independent and in it, it said bitten by the Claybug. His red hair may have played a part in it. So, that's what we began calling him.

Clay as far as growing up was a good baby. As a child you could tell him something and he would mind you. He was just an easy child, a good child all the way around. As he got older, he loved skateboarding and riding bicycles. He would go over to his grandmama's, Nanny Carolyn Page, in Calhoun Falls where he and his cousins would ride bicycles and skateboards.

Clay loved hunting and fishing. It bothered me when he went duck hunting. He would get up early in the morning and go out on a canoe across the lake. He would wear his waders. I would tell him, 'Clay, please don't put on those waders until you get to where you're hunting.' I was scared to death that the canoe would flip over, and those waders would fill with water and pull him under. He would always say, 'Mama, I know what I'm doing.' There was no changing his mind about duck hunting. He would do a little deer hunting but not a whole lot. He mostly stuck to duck hunting and fishing.

Where did Clay get his love for the great outdoors?

"Probably, a little bit from, his dad, my daddy and step daddy. Tubby Worley got him into duck hunting. He got into coon hunting with Uncle Norman. Boy are there some stories to be told about them coon hunting. They loved to torment Uncle Norman. Often, they would put stuff in his hair. They messed with his truck all the time. It hurt Clay when he lost his Papa Ricky and when he lost his Uncle Norman. They were so close. Norman had lost his whole family to illnesses. I think Clay filled that void like a son. Because of losing his family to cancer, I think having Clay around helped him through the rest of his life. I have said this often, when Norman left this world, he was with the person he loved the most."

Clay Duck Hunting

"Things work out for a reason, Clay feeling the pull to stop by and check on his Uncle Norman that day in the hospital, was nothing but God guiding him to be there with Norman."

Jennifer continues,

"He was there with his Uncle Norman when he passed. I think he has had a hard time with that, but I am glad he was there. I think Norman loved Clay more than he did anybody. Uncle Norman is responsible for getting Clay started with the guitar. He would take him to his guitar lessons in Calhoun Falls. He would pick and play. Once he started with the guitar it was the end of a lot of things, like hunting. Music became his passion.

On Wednesday nights I would go to church and then come home, and he would be set up and practicing at the house. His friends would come over and they would practice on those Wednesday nights. My garage transformed into their practice studio. I would cook supper for them. They would practice as long as they needed to practice. Many nights we would slip out there and listen to them. They would act crazy sometimes. I have pictures of their antics. I would try to line it up so that he could go play at different spots. I would load them up in my car because none could drive back then. I would take them where they needed to go.

Clay, the little red headed boy, was always so very shy. I would have never thought in a million years he would get into music and performing. He played baseball with the recreational center and was a good pitcher. He could place the ball anywhere he wanted to. It just wasn't for him. I think he stopped playing baseball when he was ten or eleven. He played basketball some at Camp Harmony. While he enjoyed those, he was never a real sports person. I never envisioned him as one who would end up in the music industry because he was so shy and timid. It amazed me when he began performing on front of people and how much courage and drive, he had. Once he decided that was what he wanted to do, he was a go getter."

Clay in Full Court Press

"To be honest he wanted to quit high school because he absolutely hated school. He struggled with school. I always wondered if he had a learning disability because he disliked it so much. He is so easily distracted and can be all over the place.

He did not like math. I tell him all the time that math is not my strong subject either and he probably got it from me. His dad was incredibly good in school as are Clay's sister and brother. I am not saying Clay isn't smart. Book smart just wasn't his thing. He didn't want it. There are two or three teachers responsible for him graduating. I tell these teachers all the time that I'm thankful they cared enough to keep pushing him.

Clay really wanted to quit his senior year. One of his teachers, Dr. Rivers sat him down and that's all it took. I told him I did not care how long he sat there, he was too close to graduation, and he was going to graduate. I had all the obstacles against me because I was a single mom in the eleventh grade when I had him. I told him, if I could do it, he could do it. Dr. Rivers and a few others were instrumental in him making it.

I realized that Clay would never attend college. Music was his dream, something he wanted to pursue. I had done everything I could for him, including booking his shows until he turned eighteen. I told him, 'All right, you're eighteen. I have two more I still must raise. You are going to have to do this yourself. I would still be there to help when I could.'

Being a single mom, I worked a lot, as many as three jobs sometimes. His dad and I had divorced, and I lost my job and then we lost our home. Clay had to grow up quickly. He had to step up and help me with my other two. I had to depend on him a lot to help me with them. I have done everything I could to make sure they have things. It was an eyeopener for him to witness how hard I have had to struggle, trying to survive, losing my job and the house.

If there was one thing that I have tried to teach them is to not give up hope and not lose your faith. Everything happens for a reason. I kept praying. I knew God had something in store for us. I never gave up on trying to come back home. It took us about seven years and then we were back home. My hope is that in the whole journey it made my kids see no matter what, do not ever give up. Believe in the Lord and keep reaching for what you want. You must have faith."

I paused, telling Jennifer that I could see that she had truly instilled this in Clay. She had accomplished just that in her journey. It had impacted his life and outlook.

"Clay lived it. I think the others may have seen it. Conner was three when we divorced. It was a rough path, figuring out things. Clay understands why we divorced. It was not a good situation. I remarried in 2011. My husband, Derrick Moon does what he can to help with my children. He is awesome. All that I had to do was ask Derrick for help and he will do what he could to help them. He reminds me a lot of my stepdad. He has gone above and beyond to help.

I think Clay had a good childhood. He, Jimmy, and Tyler were inseparable. They spent a lot of time at my home. Boy, some of things they tell me now that they did, oh my goodness. They waited until they were grown to tell me these things. Growing up, those three would always go down to the lake and go fishing, and swimming. Tyler's folks had a pool, so they would spend a lot of time there as well. Mostly they just did boy stuff, bicycling and skateboarding. When any of them walked in my door they knew they could treat my house like their own. They were that comfortable with coming here and raiding the cabinets and fridge if they wanted to. They didn't have to ask for permission. I wanted them to feel like this was there home too. I would often take them to the skating rink."

Clay at his childhood home

"I tried to be a hands-on mom. When I grew up, I didn't live with my mom. I lived with my dad. When my mom and dad divorced, I lived with her, but when my brother was killed in the automobile accident, I moved in with my dad. Daddy did not let me do a whole lot, but the things I did do probably weren't the best decisions. I always said that when I had kids and they grew up, I wanted them to have the opportunities that I had not had. If they wanted to play sports, I wanted them to be active and play sports. I have allowed all of them to choose their own paths. I am not going to lie, I wanted Clay to play baseball. I said, please play but he would say he didn't like it that well. He chose music instead. I never saw him pick up anything to make me think he was musically inclined. When he did, it shocked all of us. I go back to him always being a good kid though"

What advice, if any, would you offer Clay about his career?

"When we did the American Idol thing, it was a good opportunity for all the kids that participated. My opinion, there were plenty of kids that were denied the spotlight and the televised background stories of how they had gotten there. There was so much that the viewing audience did not see. I felt so sorry for many of them. I did not realize until Clay's experience how involved it is to do this show. I told him not waste this opportunity. Take it as a steppingstone. Just another step in the direction that you are wanting to go.

When Idol interviewed me, I was asked what I thought. I told them that everything happens for a reason. As I have always told Clay, reach for the stars, work hard, look to God, and let God place you where you need to be. If you do that, you're not going down the wrong path. Keep working at it, praying about it, keep the faith, and you're going to be where He wants you to be. You need to wait on Him. I keep telling Clay that. I told him you're not going to get where you need to be by staying here in Elberton. You have got to get out of Elberton. I told Clay he needed to be going to Nashville at least once a month and doing what he needed to do to put himself out there. It is not going to come to him here.

I am not going to say he hasn't had some rough spots and has gotten discouraged. He doesn't tell me but as a mama I can see it. I can feel it. When I sense he is having those days I sit him down and say, 'Look son. You must keep moving and keep going. Put yourself out there.' I am not crazy about him traveling. He is heading to Oklahoma in a while and I am not crazy about it. It scares me. People can be so mean out there. It worries me, him going places alone. I must remind myself, whether he is here or out there, it's not going to make a difference one way or the other. I must put my trust and faith in the good Lord. Ask for His protection over him. We get tickled with Clay a lot because he is all over the place. My mama will call me and say do you know where Clay is…and I will interrupt her and say, 'Mama, I don't know'. People will ask me where Clay is, what he is doing and I'll them, 'I don't know.' I have to check online to keep up with him.

We have gone down this path with him. What does he want to do, be a singer or a songwriter? He is conflicted. He loves to perform but he also loves to be at home. Clay is extremely family oriented. He is very close to all of us. He struggles with knowing what he needs to do but wanting to be home. He needs to be on the road. I have told my kids I just want them to be happy with whatever they are doing.

One thing I will never forget is taking Clay on his first trip to Nashville. While there we met with the Nashville Songwriters Association and a lady named Sherry. She sat Clay down and was perfectly frank with him. She asked him one question. 'Do you want to clock in everyday to a job that you dislike, or would you prefer working something you are passionate about?' When we left that meeting, I told Clay that she had made a perfectly good point. You can clock into that job everyday that you absolutely hate, or you can work some place where you have a love for doing. I told him he must make that decision as to the direction best for him. So far, the good Lord has taken care of him and has provided for him."

Do you feel good about Clay's career choice?

"I do. I cannot imagine him being as good as he is in music and doing something else. He has plenty of songs that he has written and not produced yet. At the time, they told us that if he likes something he has written, for him to place it in an envelope and mail it to himself and not open it. I have several of these in a file cabinet that he has not recorded yet. Maybe one day he will ask for them and record the songs. I just can't image Clay doing anything else than what he has chosen to do."

Like any parents after a divorce, everything is not always amicable between parties. Often power struggles can develop, pitting one against the other. Which one knows the best paths for their children? This can also lead to strained relationships, children with both or either parent. It can be intentional pitting children against one another, nor it might just be one's preference versus the others. Sadly, children are the ones paying the price and caught in the middle. Jennifer talked a bit about her relationship with her ex-husband and how it plays into raising their three children. Sometimes it feels good to get it off your chest.

Jennifer explains.

> "When Clay and I were talking about him doing his book I told him it was strange that he would mention doing his life story. I told him that I had been writing a bit about mine. My hopes are that if I complete my story, maybe my testimony will help others. Everyone has their own battle. We all face it at different times and in different ways. Clay works hard to have a good relationship with his dad. He tries to keep the peace with everyone. I sincerely want all my children to have a relationship with their dad. I encourage it.
>
> As Rodney and I went through the divorce, Clay avoided having much to do with his dad. He was stubborn, saying he just wanted to stay at home. I told all three of my children that until they are sixteen, they will spend time staying with their daddy every other weekend. I tried to make that happen. I told them once they turn sixteen and they have a car and life, it would then be their decision. Regardless as to what our differences were and what happened between us, I felt strongly about them maintaining a relationship with their dad. He and I do not see eye to eye on a lot of things, but he is still their daddy. It does not matter what happened to us and our marriage, he is their daddy. There are times when I nip it, telling them they are not going to disrespect their daddy. He may think I have been the one to try to turn them against him, but that has never been the case."

Jennifer again explained how she took on any jobs to provide for her children. Clay's Aunt Cindy Stone owned and managed the Abbeville Subway for many years. Jennifer worked for her when Clay was a young kid. The Subway is still there but the aunt is no longer affiliated with it. Jennifer wanted them to have things that she had not had growing up. She admitted that there were probably times that she failed her children along the way by not being at home more because she was working so much. She had to do what she had to do.

Jennifer continues.

> "Clay is and always has been a good kid. I am proud of him no matter what. Same goes for my other two, Gracie and Connor. When Clay first began pursuing music, Stan Brown of Stan's Music World in Elberton, told me that Clay Page sounded like a good stage name. I said to him then that I did not see that ever happening. I didn't see the typical little red-haired boy that often played for hours entertaining himself ever becoming a singer and songwriter. He loved dirt biking and four wheeling too much.
>
> He had this golden retriever named Bailey. That dog went everywhere that Clay went. If I asked Bailey where Clay was, that dog would turn his head and then walk to wherever Clay might be at the time. Bailey became extremely sick and would disappear, wanting to go off and die. I don't believe Bailey wanted us to be around him when he passed. I would tell Clay we needed to go find him. We would and we would bring him back and place him in the garage.
>
> Bailey had gotten so bad though and eventually I ended up taking him at 3 AM one morning to a 24-hour vet. I drove him there by myself. They met me at the car and took him inside while I filled out the paperwork for them euthanize him. Before I completed the paperwork, they came back and told me Bailey had already passed. I thought…that dog, he stayed alive long enough so that we were not in his presence when he passed. Even though it was hard giving

up Bailey, at least I didn't have to be the reason his heart stopped."

I shared with Jennifer that Clay had told me his mama was not one who had wanted dogs inside the house, but she had taken Bailey inside when the dog had been its sickest.

> "That's right but I loved old Bailey. Clay has two dogs now, Remi and Lilly. I have my favorite, Lilly, his golden doodle. She is precious. Her personality is special. The other dog, Remi, can be a little standoffish and more reserved and all too serious. After losing Bailey I have been cautious to not allow myself getting too close to any animals. Clay had Bailey from the time he was five until he was sixteen when he died. We have a golden retriever now, but I will not allow myself to become too attached to him. Don't let Clay fool you. I do allow Clay's dogs inside my house."

No denying it, Jennifer loves her children and has done the best she could to provide for them. She has given them the opportunity to choose the paths they wish to pursue. What's important is their happiness. She will support them with a mother's heart. She said no matter what your circumstances might be, you can take a bad situation and turn it into good. Her take is it can be done. It's just a matter of how bad you want something in life. She admitted that Clay was a mama's boy. She added that he was not embarrassed when she said this to people with him present. He would just add that he did not care and would admit he was a mama's boy in front of anyone, saying he would always be a mama's boy.

The Mama's Boy with his Mama

Clay with Sister Gracie

Clay with Brother Connor and Sister Gracie

Clay at his 7th Birthday Party

Jennifer, Clay, Gracie, and Connor

Grandmother Camilla, Clay, Jennifer and stepdad Derrick Moon

Uncle Norman Robinson, Clay, Jennifer, her dad James Robinson, Gracie, and Connor

The Miracle Child

Camilla is Clay's grandmother, Jennifer's mom. She resides in Powdersville, South Carolina, in Anderson County. Camilla had been married to James first and then to Ricky. She admitted that the Clay subject matter was one of her favorite topics. Remember, she is the grandmother who has supported Clay financially as well as giving him support and a caring shoulder when needed. Camilla has often been Clay's sounding board sometimes offering him advice about the endeavors haunting him.

Camilla reminisced about living in Calhoun Falls for a while. Her parents had moved there when she was five. She had grown up there. She married her first husband, James Robinson just across the Savannah River in Georgia. They had three children and had lost two. Jennifer is her surviving child. Her daughter was only three days old when the newborn died from amniotic pneumonia. Her son Michael was three years old at the time. In 1974 they had no real cure for amniotic pneumonia. Today her daughter would have survived. Her son Michael was sixteen when he died in an automobile accident on the way to school one morning. Camilla credits God with giving her three grandchildren. She says Jennifer has been a wonderful mother.

Camilla begins.

> "The day Clay was born was one of the happiest days of mine and his Papa Ricky's life. I had lost my son, Michael, in a car accident. I still have Clay's mother, Jennifer, but there will always be a void in my life due to the loss of my son. When that little boy arrived in the world, it helped fill some of that void. Ricky and I have no children together. We kept Clay a lot. Jennifer, being a young mother prompted us to keeping him many times when I was off work during the week and some weekends. He was such a joy. Clay was the easiest baby and as a little boy he was so laid back and easy going. He was such a good child. We could take him to a restaurant or anywhere, and he was always well behaved. He was just a sweet, sweet child. When he was older, I would get him about one weekend a month and it would be his weekend. We went out to eat and

his choice was almost always Ryans Steak House and we always made a trip to Chuckie Cheese. Fun times!

I remember when he was about three or four months old, he was having what we thought was colic. My baby sister refused to keep him, saying she would not keep that child because his breathing was not right. She added that he grunts a lot, something just was not quite right. He had been taken to the doctor several times, but they hadn't detected anything abnormal other than saying it was colic.

On one occasion we had been in Elberton shopping. Clay was in the back seat. We had planned to pick up some medicine for the colic. While Jennifer was inside the store, I was watching him. Clay stopped breathing. I grabbed him out of the car seat and ran inside the store with him. By then, he had begun breathing again. We took him to the Abbeville emergency room. They began performing all kinds of tests on him. The next we knew they had him onboard an ambulance and heading to Greenwood, a larger hospital in the next county in South Carolina.

There, they put Clay on oxygen. They diagnosed him with Group B Strep. This was highly unusual for a child his age. It is contracted during birth. The mother is normally a carrier but unaware that she is. Typically, a doctor will prescribe the mother with antibiotics and it protects the child. No one knew though. Most of the time the strep shows up within hours of the birth. It's not unusual for babies to die with this strep. The doctor told us that Clay was septic. They said they would do their best to turn it around, adding he was not out of the woods. He remained in the hospital for about eleven days on strong antibiotics. So strong, we could smell the antibiotics on his skin. They managed to turn it around and cure him. From that point moving forward Jennifer took antibiotics before she gave birth to her other children."

Camilla proudly explains.

> "Clay was our miracle baby. The doctors found it difficult to believe that he had lived this long with it. If not detected in time, death is the common outcome. He was God's gift all the way around; not that Jennifer's other two weren't. They are too but Clay just arrived under unusual circumstances. He was such a beautiful sweet child. We could not take him anywhere without someone going on about him. When we were in the hospital there were nurses from other floors dropping by to see him. They wanted to see the miracle baby."

Moving forward, Camilla expanded on life with young Clay.

> "Ricky and I were into four wheelers. We both had one. Clay and his friend Tyler had little four-wheelers as well. We and Tyler's grandparents would often take those boys with us to ride. They were good riders, but we would keep them from getting hurt by positioning them between us. They loved riding fast and this prevented them from taking off ahead of us. Tyler's papa and Ricky's wisdom prevailed. We would go over to my husband's mother's home. She was crazy about Clay. She would sit out on the front porch in the summertime and read to him. She was thrilled that Clay played country music. It was her favorite. So, when Nanny Irene became ill and was on her death bed, Clay came and sat beside her bed and played his guitar for her.
>
> There was also some acreage next to her place belonging to Mr. John Owens, He would allow us to make trails and ride on his land. A group of men came up from Atlanta to visit Mr. Owens and we became friends with them. One night we built a bonfire. We took Clay with us to roast marshmallows. Clay would call them 'washmellers'. One of the older gentlemen, Don, asked, 'What did he just say?' Clay said it again. Don then said, 'Clay, it's not washmellers. It's marshmallows.' He made Clay say it several times. I told Don that he was ruining my sweet baby because it was so cute how he said it.

> We took Clay riding everywhere, including trails in Greenwood and Abbeville Counties. We even went to Waycross, Georgia. We had a wonderful time with Clay. As a child, if he ever started fighting sleep, I could always put him on the riding lawnmower with his Papa Ricky. After about two turns around the yard Clay would be asleep. The noise didn't bother him. He would fall asleep every time. We would take him with us fishing in our boat. I think he might have caught his first fish while fishing with us. I recall how neat. He was so tickled and such a little fellow. We let him pull that fish in by himself. I think it was a crappie. After Clay was grown, my husband took him on a trip to Santee Cooper. He thoroughly enjoyed it, showing Clay the lake, and how large the fish were there."

Camilla talks about how she used to be quite athletic growing up, playing softball and basketball. She was excited when Clay took a shine to baseball.

> "When Clay began playing baseball, I would play catch with him. I was much younger then and I would run to second and third base, and then have him throw the ball to me. He was a great fielder and pitcher. Clay could put that ball anywhere he wanted to and always hit the target. He was that good.
>
> He eventually decided he loved music better. I recall coming home one night and Clay was with us in the backseat of our car. He had already begun playing the guitar at this point. My husband loved country music and he was playing a song. When it would finish Clay would say. 'Play it again, Papa.' Ricky would play the song again. Clay would say, 'Play it again, Papa.' He would play it again. After about the fourth or fifth time, Clay began strumming his guitar and playing the song. Ricky looked at me and I looked at him. We were awe struck. He had just sat back there and listened a few times and then went with it. Clay does not read music. He plays by ear. He's just a natural."

Camilla brought up a familiar name, Uncle Norman and explained the relationship Clay had with him.

> "Clay went to his Uncle Norman's. Norman had lost his entire family. My kids and then Jennifer and Rodney's became his. He enjoyed Clay. Norman took an interest in him and his music. He wanted Clay to get better at it. Norman took Clay to Calhoun Falls to a man to take lessons."

I interrupted Camilla, telling her I had interviewed Vernon Brown, the man she was referencing, and told her how I had worked with Vernon and his wife for nearly twenty years. She continued.

> "I told Clay that I played piano. I wasn't good at it, but I did play. I had taken lessons for about two years. I also had played the flute in the high school band. I told Clay that I could read music. I confessed that I wished I could play by ear like him. My older sister could but I could not. I told Clay, the difference between him and me was that he understood music in the fiber of his being and how it was ingrained in him. I can read the music and play it by what I see. Clay feels it. It is a gift. Clay is amazing. He can hear something and then take off with it. He can sit around, and it will pop inside his head, and he will take off with it."

I mentioned to Camilla that Clay had shared with me about how she had financially supported him at times with his music or when times were hard. She acknowledged this.

> "His Papa Ricky and I were able to help him. We were able to finance a lot of things for him. If Ricky found out that Clay needed a piece of equipment, he would try his best to get it for him. Ricky bought Clay his first car. (the now infamous Isuzu Rodeo). We knew he was going to start traveling and Ricky said he wanted him to be safe. We did what we could to help him.
>
> I recall there was this gentleman that had an Ibanez guitar for sale. Ricky found out about it. He asked if the man would sell it to him for his grandson. Ricky gave the man

one of Clay's CDs. After he listened to it, he contacted Ricky and told him he would not sell the guitar to him. Instead, he gave it to Ricky saying he wanted him to give it to Clay. He said he wanted him to tell Clay to use it, that he was gifted. I wish that I could recall the man's name. He was a friend of my deceased husband. Ricky told Clay when he gave him that guitar to keep it on his bed and before he climbed in bed each night, he wanted him to play on it some, practice before he set it down.

Ricky worked for a custom builder. He met a lot of people on his job. Ricky started working when he was ten years old. I know some might wonder about that, but it was true. He has always been a worker. I have known Ricky to dig post holes all day long for a friend for just twenty dollars. Ricky loved people and enjoyed helping people. He loved his grandchildren. They were not step-grandchildren to him. They were his grandchildren. He made sure Jennifer had a washer and dryer and microwave when Clay was a baby. He loved doing for others.

We attended every Clay show that we could get to, no matter how far away they were. We drove to Alabama one time. There was a gentleman with Clay there, but he could not stay. He needed to return home to go to work. Ricky and I loaded him and his belongings in our car and took him back to Elberton. Then we returned to Alabama to watch Clay.

Camilla discusses Ricky's passing.

"Clay dropped by the hospital shortly after I had been told by the doctor that there was nothing more that they could medically do for Ricky's cancer. Clay showing up caught me by surprise because he was not supposed to come from Elberton to Greenville, S.C. on his return trip to Nashville. Normally he would take the route through Atlanta. I asked, 'Clay, why are you here? You're supposed to be on your way back to Nashville.' He said, 'I know. Something told me to come here, to come this way.' I had been sitting there reading my bible. Clay looked at me and asked what was wrong. I had to tell him. I told Clay how proud his papa was of him and that we only had a few days left with him. I told him I knew Ricky was not blood kin and Cay stopped me in mid-sentence and said, 'Oh he is. That man lying in that bed is an example of what every man ought to be.' He then walked over and grabbed his papa's hand. While holding it he took a picture with his phone of just their hands before saying. 'Papa, I'm going to Nashville to do this recording and it's going to have your name on it. I'm then coming back because I want you to hear it.'

When Clay got ready to leave, he started out the door slowly. It must have taken what seemed like five minutes, him looking back, eventually through the crack in the door. All I could see was him getting smaller and smaller until I could only see his eyes peering through it. He later told me that it was the worst trip he had ever taken. He called me that next morning and said, 'Nanny, I'm on my way back.' I told him, 'Clay it was supposed to take you two days to do your recordings.' He said he had completed it in two rough drafts. He wanted his papa to hear it. He was so afraid that his papa was going to pass before he had a chance to hear it. He made it back in time and played it for him. When it was released, on the inside cover of the CD it had in memory of Ricky Haggerty."

Graduation Day with Papa Ricky and Grandmother Camilla

Camilla explained that Clay was special to a lot of people. She said she has never witnessed such an outpouring of love to a young man who was struggling and trying to make it. She laughed, adding every time she and Ricky went to where Clay was playing, people referred to them as Clay's roadies. Ricky often helped Clay unload and set up his equipment. It was commonplace for people to approach Camilla and have nice things to say about Clay.

> "Over and over people would ask me why someone hasn't grabbed him up yet? Why doesn't he have a record deal? He has a gift. Someone should take notice. Clay has the total package, the looks, the talent, the stage presence. He does not have a powerhouse voice, but he has a good voice, better than some of the artist that have already made it. I

think he has it all. He can write his own music. He can master the lyrics."

I asked Camilla my typical question. What would you like to see Clay do with his career, be a songwriter or a performer?

"I think he can do both. He has the capability to do either. What I want for him, and I say this prayer all the time, is that God will put the right people in his life to lead him the right way, to mentor him the right way, and take him to where he needs to be. Clay made this statement to me after Ricky's funeral, 'Nanny, when I saw the kind of people that my papa surrounded himself with, Godly people, my respect for him grew.' I told him that this was what I prayed for him. I told him that if he had taken the path of alcohol and drugs and a life going down the drain, I would rather him drive a trash truck the rest of his life.

Clay is not above doing what needs to be done to make ends meet. I regret that Ricky is no longer around to be in his brother Connor's life. Ricky always gave the boys advice. When it came to hunting Ricky would say if you're not going to eat it, don't kill it. You eat what you kill. It makes me so grateful when Clay does reach out to me and ask my opinion. I feel maybe that's why God still has me here, for me to be here for my daughter and my grandchildren when they need me. I was older than Ricky. I often questioned why him first, but Ricky let me know that he wouldn't swap places with me.

I remember once going to a bar in Laurens, S.C. where Clay was about to play. When we walked inside, we saw something near the stage, and I asked Ricky what it was. Ricky walked over and checked it out. He returned and told me it was a steel cage. I guess they could pull it around the performers if things got too rowdy to protect those on stage. This wasn't chicken wire like you see in the movies. It was the real deal.

Ricky and I made plenty of trips with Clay, including biker bars. Some of the best people in the world are bikers. They were so supportive of him. He met a lot of people in Tennessee when he started his song writing. I remember the first time we walked down Nashville's Music Row and how awe inspiring it was for Clay. He had never been there before. I left there thinking, one day…one day…he would be there for real.

Camilla thinks, like most, that Clay should spend more time in Nashville. Camilla continues.

"Clay and I went to Nashville to meet with an attorney. He was trying to decide if he should sign with a managing group. We spent an entire afternoon with him, a genuinely nice gentleman. He told Clay that he didn't have to move back to Nashville, but he suggested he return at least one week monthly to allow people to see him and hear him. Clay has developed a lot of connections there as well as receiving recognition from a few important people. Clay had planned a trip in April to go on tour across country. He would have been gone the entire month. When he makes up his mind to do something, he does it, however, due to Covid-19, the tour was cancelled. That year he spent in Nashville he was lonely, but he stuck it out, made himself do what needed to be done. He got out and made the rounds to meet people. He put himself out there for people to see. He came home almost every weekend but during the week he was faithfully there doing what needed to be done."

Camilla mentioned a familiar name, Tubby Worley, saying how close he was to Clay. She said Clay looks up to Tubby as well.

"Tubby had taken Clay under his wings, not having any children himself. I believe he absolutely loves Clay and wants only the best for him. He and his brother Zeb have tried to help and mentor Clay. They have been phenomenal in Clay's life. There have been so many people instrumental in his life who have helped him. There was this one guy we met at a biker bar; he and his wife are very nice people. He told Clay that if he would go and try to compete on The Voice, he would give him a thousand dollars to help get him started. At that time though, Clay was much younger and had not quite figured what he wanted to do. Idol was a blessing when it came along. We laugh about it now how it just came out of the blue; that Papa Ricky must have whispered in God's ear. Ricky always wanted him to succeed."

As I do with any interviews I dug deep for the dirt. I asked Camilla if she had any of those odd or funny stories worth sharing.

"Did anyone tell you about them setting the woods on fire?"

This was a favorite one indeed, having heard about it from Clay and Jennifer. It probably was not that funny back then though.

> "Clay, Tyler and Jimmy always enjoyed picking on Uncle Norman. They loved him but they kept something going all the time. They pulled all sorts of things on him. Once, during the middle of the night, they decided to get up and try to scare him. They climbed on top of his house and began walking around on the roof. They woke him up doing it.
>
> No denying it though, if there was anyone that Norman would have wanted to be with him when he passed, it would have been Clay. Clay was his heart. I told Clay after it happened, how hard it had to have been on him, but of all the people who could have been there Norman would have wanted him. He had received a tug as he passed the hospital and he turned around and came back. Clay said something just told him to. Had he not listened to that presence in his heart, he would not have been there. I am so proud of Clay because so many times when he is performing, he will make sure to give God thanks. He will tell people that God has been good to him.
>
> I don't know if anyone has told you about his friend, Brad Evans. They play together some. When they are together and performing, they are hilarious. I recently told Clay that they reminded me of Dean Martin and Jerry Lewis when they performed. Brad is always saying stuff about Clay and Clay plays the role of the straight man. People just crack up

> at their antics. Sometimes Clay's face turns as red as his hair, but he just goes along with it. Picking and grinning."

Camilla again claims that Clay is a good grandson, adding that if she had to go out into the world and pick one, she could not have picked a better first grandchild. She mentioned how they had always called him Claybug as well. She recalled the article in the paper about people who did sculptures and in bold headlines it said **Bit by the Claybug**. One memory can jar another. Camilla shared this one.

> "I remember this one time when Clay got a bit sassy with me. I told him I was going to spank him. I had never spanked him before. He was maybe ten. I had a belt and I had him bend over. I popped him. He looked at me and grinned and said, 'That didn't hurt.' So, I popped him again. This time a little harder. He said, 'Oops.' I got his attention then after putting a little more effort in it. It was so funny, his reaction. That was it. I was done. He was such a good kid I did not often have to discipline him. He couldn't fib though. We could tell. We knew when he was up to something. All we would have to say was 'Clay.' He was not a very good deceitful child.
>
> Clay has tried to learn as much as he can from his Papa James. There is nothing that man cannot build or fix. He is a wealth of knowledge and world of information. James and Clay built Clay's tiny house. James is a good man, just a quiet man."

If you could sit Clay down today, what grandmotherly advice would you give him about life, career, relationships?

> "As far as his and Maggie's relationship, Maggie has been there for him all through this. She has supported him. She is smart. She has done what she has needed to do to further his career. She gets him to where he needs to be. Very little does she complain. She loves him. I know that and I know he loves her. If it is God's will for her to be with him' that's what I want as well.

Clay called me the other day from Nashville. I told him he did not have to be in a hurry to make decisions. This is your life. Take time. Pray about it. I have always told him to ask for God's direction. If you listen to God's direction, He wants what is best for you. And whatever He chooses for you, it is going to be the best thing that could ever possibly happen to you and for you. We make a lot of mistakes in life by not listening to that inner voice that God puts within us. Based on a lot of the little perks he has gotten from time to time, I know Clay has that little voice inside him. I have seen the respect and the admiration he has for the veterans that have served this country. He has made a point to visit VA homes. We have told him he must learn to be a role model; that he has kids and young people watching him.

Clay's brain is constantly thinking. He is into this, into that. I think he might be a little bit ADHD and maybe he gets that from me. He's so smart and has such a sense of entrepreneurship. He has done well, managing his career. I think he needs more of a booking agent than a manager. By the same token, managing himself takes up a lot of his time. If Clay could find someone that he trusted who could make the right decisions for him, I'm all for it. Clay refers to it like handing your baby off to someone else."

There are so many documented horror stories of agents and managers who have taken advantage of their clients; clients who trusted them and then were ultimately betrayed. Celebrities who had it all, or thought they did, only to find out they had been bilked out of their fortune by the very one that was supposed to be preserving and protecting their livelihood and investments. Relinquishing ownership is a tough decision, one that should never be taken lightly and one that should be weighed with caution. It's not difficult understanding Clay's dilemma in making this leap.

Camilla shares more memories.

"Clay was playing at a venue. There was another gentleman there who had made it relatively far in one of the singing competitions. Clay said to me, 'Nanny, I couldn't believe how arrogant he was. I don't ever want to be like that.' After Idol, he came to me and said, 'I want to ask you something. Do you think I'm arrogant?' I laughed and said no. He then said, 'Well, I never want to be.' His mom and I both have told him if he gets too big for his britches, we would let him know. We were in a restaurant in Anderson eating supper. The waiter brought our drink order and then asked, 'Are there any paparazzi outside?' Clay looked puzzled, grinning, he said, 'No.' When the waiter left, Clay turned to Maggie and asked, 'What did he mean?' We laughed and told him that someone had recognized him as a celebrity. We have always told him to never forget where he came from, to not forget his roots and never forget who he is. I never want him to lose himself in what is taking place.

I have had so many people come to me where we were watching him perform and say that he is so approachable or he's so humble. That's what people like about him. He always reminds me that he is a mama's boy; that he will always be a mama's boy. I cannot recall who, but some celebrity did confess to Clay that they were a mama's boy. I guess that opened him up to admitting he was one as well. He is grandmama's boy too. His brother and sister have said that Clay is the golden child. I defend that by telling them they don't understand that I don't love him anymore than I love them, but he came along at a time in my life when I need him. He filled an empty spot in my heart. We almost lost him too. He gave a richness to Ricky's and my marriage that otherwise would not have been there. We were able to nurture Clay and watch that baby grow up and be part of this life. We did the same with the other two as well. Clay was just the first one.

Clay has met so many people throughout his life that have helped him and have been a blessing to him. He thinks the world of Benji Greeson at the Abbeville radio station.

You can learn valuable lessons by talking with the mothers and grandmothers of people. No denying it, in this family God is the center piece. Prayer and trusting in God's signs and guidance have never loomed larger. Giving thanks to Him for all he does is important. It might be tough for Clay to hand over the steering wheel to a managing firm but there is no hesitation in allowing God to navigate the highway to his future. God is indeed good and life with Him in Clay's life can only result in a wonderful ending. The journey has many miles to go yet but no doubt it will be a memorable experience for Clay and those who love and support him. They are weak but He is strong; yes, Jesus loves them, for the Bible tells us so.

Making a Difference
When a Difference Counts Most

Rodney is Clays dad. Born and raised in Calhoun Falls, South Carolina he graduated from Calhoun Falls High School. Rodney begins,

> "I was nineteen when Clay was born. His mother was seventeen. We started out as young parents. We had to grow up very quickly. Clay witnessed his mother and me as we had to struggle for most everything we had. He did not lack in love. We were there with him. We did not get married until he was about three years old. We didn't want a mistake to be the reason we got married. He was twelve when we divorced. I think that had a bearing on him. I think that led to him resent me. I always prayed that in his adult life he would understand that I was doing the best for the family, me leaving. His mother and I just could not get along. I hope I am not going to deep in my thoughts. I think I left Clay at a vulnerable time in his life. My decision was based on my thinking I was going to do more harm than good trying to make it work. We had a broken relationship that could not be repaired.
>
> Clay and I did a lot of hunting and fishing together. I would like to say he got his love of music from me. I was always a southern rock and classic rock kind of guy. I don't play any instruments and can barely play the radio, but he learned music by hearing what I listened to.
>
> I bought Clay a $99 guitar, a New York Pro from Stan's Music World in Elberton for his ninth birthday. Except for the time he had mono and spent a few days in the hospital, I think he has picked up a guitar every day of his life since I bought him that guitar. His Uncle Norman, who was a big influence on him, taught him his first few chords. He signed him up with a local guy in Calhoun Falls, Vernon Brown, for lessons. He has been hooked ever since. I don't think I would be lying by saying that.

Clay is persistent in what he does. He really believes in what he does. In the early going his mother and I struggled for everything we had. We did not have anything given to us. I considered us as being lower middle class back then. Doing better now but at ages nineteen and seventeen we didn't have much experience at being adults. Clay witnessed us struggling to make ends meet. I think we provided well considering the circumstances. He was shown a lot of love, but I think he learned some of his work ethics by watching his mother and me struggle."

How would you describe your relationship with Clay now?

"I never said anything bad about his mother in front of him. I think Clay probably sided with his mother though when I left. The situation was both our faults, partly mine and partly hers. I never felt Clay needed the burden of having to choose sides. I always tried to stay in the shadows and allow him to form an opinion about me without asking his mom. I always prayed that some day he might see my side of the story. Recently, probably less than a year ago, Clay approached me and told me 'Daddy, I want you to know that I see your side of things now since growing up.' He just needed to figure this out on his own. He has come a long way. I believe our relationship is great now. He was twelve years old when I left and when he graduated high school, I think he held a lot of resentment toward me.

Not that he has told me, but I think he had a lot of questions for me and some pent resentment because of it. All he saw and remembers is that I just up and left them without an explanation. I just felt at the time that it was better left unsaid. No lying about it, his mother and I had some verbal arguments that he was witness to, but there was nothing physical to them. We were just kids and had a difficult time getting along. We did make it last five years and had two more beautiful children. It was a busted relationship that was not repairable. I think back now and believe we would both agree that it was the best thing that we went our separate ways."

Do you have any favorite hunting or fishing stories about Clay?

"I was with Clay when he killed his first deer. I remember buying him a '308' rifle for Christmas when he was maybe eight years old. He was always afraid to shoot it until I took him over to my brother's house to sight it in for him. My brother's daughter is about six months older than Clay. We finished sighting it in and had it hitting close. My brother asked his daughter if she wanted to shoot it. She said yeah. After she shot it, Clay knew then that he had to shoot it too. He did not want to, but he knew since she had, he had to as well. He sucked it up and wrapped a couple of extra coats around his shoulder before he would though. I told him if he would just shoot it one time that he we want to shoot the entire box of bullets. He was close to crying, but he shot it and then shot it several more times. From then on, we hunted a lot. We were part of a hunting club.

He could not stand loud noises and wore these earmuffs. I remember taking him to the Monster Jam, the first one that they had been held in Greenville at the BILO center. He was scared to death and kept his hands over his ears the whole time. He did not realize how loud those vehicles were going to be. Clay just hated loud noises. I would bet that he is still scared to death of a thunderstorm.

We lived near Hwy 72 Marine. I was working second shift at Flexible Technologies in Abbeville at the time. His mom was at work and it was the middle of day. I was just lying around when a terrible storm came up. We were living in a little mobile home. I tried not to scare him, but it was time to get out of that mobile home. We were traveling across the Lake Russel Bridge between Calhoun Falls and Georgia and the wind was blowing my little Toyota truck all over the place. I must admit, it was scaring me to death. I think it really scared him as well, causing him to be terrified of storms after that day.

I have another funny story that causes Clay to roll his eyes every time I tell it. I have always enjoyed, and still do, looking for Indian arrowheads. I would take Clay with me to hunt for arrowheads and Indian artifacts. We had bought land from his mother's family. It had been in the family forever. Back then, people would throw their junk in the woods. There was this old discarded toilet there. Clay saw it and told me, 'Look, Daddy, there's an old Indian toilet out there.' I didn't tell him otherwise but laughed about him thinking that. I will take that memory to my grave. It was such a priceless funny moment."

Did you ever go coon hunting with Uncle Norman?

Laughing, Rodney said,

"No. I never did with Norman. Coon hunting was a first and last trip for me though. I went once with my uncle before Clay was born. I vowed that night after chasing those dogs until the early morning that I would never go coon hunting again. It was two trips in one, my first and my last. Clay spent a lot of time with me in the woods and on the boat fishing. We did a lot of fishing together. Over the years we have gotten away from it.

Coming up though, it was a tradition for us to go Crappie fishing on Good Friday. It was not a holiday for me where I worked but I would take the day off. Clay and I would then go fishing. If it fell on a school day, I would let him play hooky."

My granddad always called it wetting hooks and drowning worms.

"Yep. It beats a day at work anytime."

What do you think about Clay now? You mentioned you bought him his first guitar and Uncle Norman helped him out as well. What do you think about where he is now?

"I am just so proud of his persistence and ambition, chasing his dream. I am so proud of his God given talent. He has such great work ethics. That's something to be said for his generation."

Is there any advice that you would give him about his career or life any general?

"Just something that I have always told him; be himself. Especially in music. You don't want to change for anybody. Do what you love. Do what you know. It's just the way I feel about it. Clay is so humble. He doesn't consider himself famous, but a lot of people look up to him. He has a genuine heart of gold He goes to schools and reads for kids. Parents that I work with are always showing me photographs of Clay with their children; times when he had ventured to an elementary school and read stories for the children. He always tries to give back. He might not have a lot to contribute from a monetary perspective but in his heart and soul you will never meet a humbler and more giving person.

I grew up in Abbeville County and have lived in this area here my entire life, however, I had never been inside the Abbeville Opera House on the town square until Clay performed there recently. He ended up giving them a show and playing much longer than her had intended The Opera House was beautiful. The acoustics were so great. I regret that it has taken me so many years to step foot inside it. When I was a kid, living in Calhoun Falls, we would fork out five dollars for gas and drive to Abbeville, and we would cut the town square and cruise all day long.

Clay is so talented. I am extremely proud of him. I think living the life he has lived has been inspirational for his music and his song writing. I love a singer-songwriter. You know it's a good song when another artist sings the song someone else has written and can make it their own. Uncle Norman is in one of his songs. He loved his Uncle Norman and his Uncle Norman loved him.

I don't know if anyone has mentioned his old dog, Bailey. The dog was a birthday present. We gave him that Golden Retriever in a box. That dog followed him everywhere, chasing him on his four-wheeler. Clay was always going somewhere with Norman. We lived right across the street from him. Clay would walk over and hang out with him. When Clay would ride off somewhere with Norman, Bailey would lay under Norman's porch and not move all day until they returned. Bailey was his dog and that Clay loved him. We all love our dogs. They are our babies. Bailey lived a long life; a boy and his dog."

Clay, Rodney, Connor and Gracie

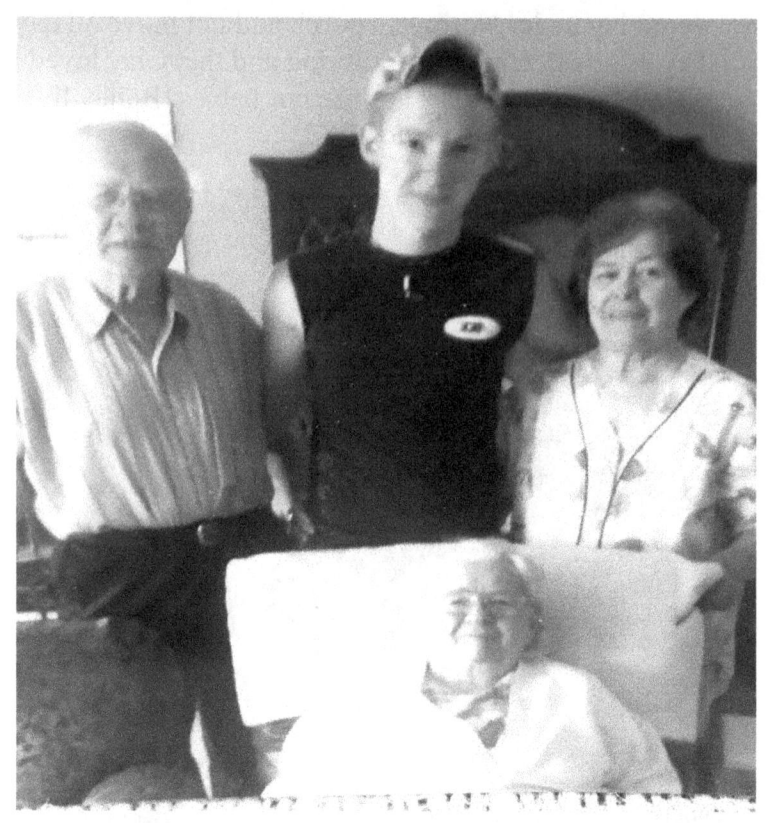

**Rodney's side of the family
Papa Parker, Clay, Nanny Carolyn
and Ma-Ma**

Mister Fix It

Clay's granddaddy, James is Jennifer's dad, Camilla's ex-husband, Uncle Norman's brother and he has quite the reputation. As reputations go, James has earned his honestly and deservingly so. Family have shared stories about his ability to fix and build just about anything. He resides along the same neck of the woods as does Jennifer, Derrick, Connor and Gracie, and Clay and Maggie. One big happy family thrive lakeside in the Georgia countryside.

Being familiar with the area, I asked James if he did any fishing. He said he used to, but after they built the lake near and around his property, he had lost interest in it. I figured he probably had some wonderful stories to share about his grandson, Clay,

James begins,

> "Clay has always seemed like more of a son to me because I lost my son when he was sixteen years old, killed in an automobile accident while on his way to school one morning. When Clay came along about that time, he just seemed more like a son than a grandson growing up around us. He was always a little bitty thing. By the time I got home from work he would be sitting across the road at my house waiting on me to get home. He seemed to always have a bicycle or some toy for me to work on. He kept me busy, always having something he wanted me to do.
>
> Clay had a skateboard that he used to ride all the time. I bet he put a hundred miles on it riding it up and down the road. He called himself being like these people you see who skate off those large ramps, so he asked me to build him one. He had an idea how he wanted it, so I built him the ramp from some metal pipe and plyboard. He would get on that thing at his mama's house and would ride up on it from the sidewalk and then jump back off it. Seeing him do that, I thought what in the world have I done; built something he is was going to hurt himself on. He enjoyed it.
>
> Next thing I knew he had dragged that ramp down to the lake. He and some of his friends had positioned it on the

lake bank. They placed lifejackets on their bicycles and would ride them down the hill and jump the bikes into the lake. They fastened those lifejackets to their bicycles so they wouldn't sink in the lake. Later I noticed I hadn't seen the bicycles, so I asked Clay about it. He said he didn't know. I think the Corp of Engineers caught them doing it and might have taken their bicycles. He never did tell me what happened to them. He and Jimmy Jones and some of his other buddies were always into something.

I have heard the story a couple of times about them setting the woods on fire.

"Oh yeah. It was one Saturday evening that he and little Jimmy Jones were down the road shooting fireworks. It was so dry that summer. I was out in the yard and could hear them shooting the fireworks down near the lake. They finally came back to the house. I later noticed a lot of smoke. I took off running down there and the whole woods were on fire. I returned and yelled to Clay that they better put out that fire. Clay said, 'What fire?' I said, 'The one y'all must have set.' They dragged water hoses from everywhere and finally put out the fire. If they hadn't it would have burned up all the woods in the area. I could tell it had scared Clay and Jimmy too.

Clay was always into something. He had a four-wheeler when he couldn't have been any older than seven or eight if he was that old. One day he was riding it out behind my house where there are a lot of deep gullies trying to jump them. I warned him to be careful on it and the next thing I heard was him crying down there. He had flipped the four-wheeler over and ended up underneath it. I seem to remember he ended up breaking his arm. He was something, a daredevil.

Bailey, his dog always followed him up and down the road while he was riding it. That dog had more mileage on him than that four-wheeler. Clay and Maggie have two dogs now that are more like kids than dogs. They don't call them dogs; they call them girls. You'll hear them saying, 'Come on girls.' I owned a chihuahua once but after it died, I said I did not want another one."

Speaking of dogs, did you ever go coon hunting with Uncle Norman?

"I went one or two times and he broke me. He broke me from every wanting to go again. I was really young then but after I got a little older, I told him I didn't see any sense in it. I just couldn't get into that coon hunting. You never know where those dogs are going to take you and it is usually so cold, and it is too dark to see anything. It just wasn't for me. Norman had Clay were all into coon hunting for a while. Clay used to love it. I think he learned the same lesson as he got a little older, how it was rough work."

They told me they were always pulling something on poor Uncle Norman. What about you, did they ever try pulling pranks on you?

"No, can't say they ever did. They usually listened to me. Guess it might have been because I was always helping Clay with his projects. I would try to teach him while helping him. You know how kids are these days; they have their minds set on one thing and are not interested in learning stuff that can help them in life.

When Clay got his little house, it wasn't much more than just a hull. I reckon it was just the two of us that did about all the work on it. He would show me what he wanted, and I would tell him let's get in there and lay it out. Clay did the sheet rock and did a good job. He surprised me. We had already worked another project for him in Elberton, his recording studio. It used to be a bathroom type business and the section he was going to use was sort of where a display unit had occupied. We added some rooms to it, extending walls to the ceiling. We made the recording studio he wanted, even carpeted the floor. It turned out much better than expected. We finished it and the next thing I knew he had decided to leave for Nashville. After we did all that work, he decided he wanted to go to Nashville. All that went down the drain."

What do you think about Clay and his music?

> "I think he is doing really good. He can't get out there now because of this virus messing everything up. He was doing good before it started."

"James, do you play music?"

> "No, sure don't. I wish I could. I have always liked music and once thought I would like to learn how to play a guitar, but I never could do it. I think Clay took it after Norman. He always played the guitar. I had another brother besides Norman that could play as well. Norman was my oldest brother. Of all the boys and girls in my family I'm the last one. Norman thought Clay was his kid too. Clay spent a lot of time with him.
>
> Clay has a sister and brother that are real close to me but Clay grew up more around us before they came along. After I lost my boy he just seemed to figure right in and take his place. He came along at the right time for that. Clay was named after my son. My boy was James Michael and he is Michael Clayton."

Readers know my routine by now. James, if you could give Clay any advice, what would you tell him?

> "All I would tell him would be to keep his head straight and stay out of the crazy mess a lot of them get into. Pick the straight line. Too many musicians get into drugs. I told Clay that when he made it big, he needed to stay like he is now. I told him just because you make a little money don't go out and spend it on everything. Try to stay like you are and drive your old car or truck. You don't have buy a bunch of stuff to be somebody."

I told James I had the stories about the Rodeo with 300,000 miles on it.

> "He has parked the Rodeo now. He said the doors felt as if they were not closing right. The windows wouldn't let up and down and the air conditioning has stopped working. The Rodeo was running hot one time, so he left it with me to look at it. I ended up replacing the water pump. I don't know if there is anything worse than trying to replace the water pump on an Isuzu. In some of these new cars you can't even find the sparkplugs in them. He is now driving a 1992 Ford truck. He just brought it over to me today and left it because he was having problems with the starter. This was what he used to drive before the Isuzu. He had been fixing it back up, just adding tires, getting a tag and insurance for it. He likes it because it has a working air conditioner.
>
> He took that Rodeo Isuzu places I would never have gone in it. I would have been afraid to. He would drive to Nashville and think nothing of it. I was proud of him when he went on American Idol. I think he could have gone further in the competition, but he was concerned about signing a contract with them. Once you do that you are stuck with them.
>
> As a kid growing up, Clay never could be still. I would never have thought he would turn out to be what he is now because was just a little skinny, shy kid. I never pictured him getting into music. As quiet as he always was, I would have never pictured him getting in front of anybody singing."

I mentioned to James that I thought Norman had been the one who had pushed Clay into performing at the Calhoun Falls Town Wide Yard Sale.

> "Clay sure liked going to yard sales. I remember him buying a puppy once while at a yard sale. He bought it for $10 and when he got home, he sold it to his sister Gracie for $5. The dog is still alive at about 12 or 13 years old."

That was downhill business losing $5 on the dog. James, you needed to spend more time teaching him finance than fixing stuff.

> "I guess Clay figured he would still be there with the dog if he sold to her, might as well make back some of the money."

James and I talked about Vernon Brown and Clay having taken lessons from him. He knows Vernon but had not seen him in a while. I told James about Vernon still driving a truck that he was driving when he and I worked together many years ago, and how he and Clay had something in common; musicians putting a lot of miles on their vehicles.

> "I can't pick a guitar, but I still have an old truck. Mine is a 1963 Ford that I bought in 1965. It had about 37,000 miles on it when I bought it. It's like that Isuzu and probably has over 300,000 miles on it now."

I know where Clay gets it from now.

> "I figured I would keep it and maybe one of the grandkids will get it one of these days. At least I hope they will want it and do something with it. I still drive it, but I don't have insurance on it. I start it up occasionally. I also have a 1974 Ford pickup truck and a 1985 Cutlass Oldsmobile. Jennifer tells me I should get rid of all this mess. I tell her I am going to keep it, might need it some day or somebody else might need it. No need getting rid of something when somewhere down the road you may have use for it."

A 1963 Ford with over 300,000 miles on it sounds like the perfect vehicle for Clay Page, one he would not be afraid to drive anywhere.

Let it Shine

The following line is from Clay's 'Let It Shine' song.

Girl I'm learning each and every day of who you are and who I am.

Clay begins,

> "I tell people I believe I have grown more in the last two years than I have in my entire life. Doing this book has given me some clarity. Plus, it's wonderful to have someone like Maggie that understands me. We share a transparent relationship, both with goals and ambitions, each supporting the other. She works hard as a teacher and as cheerleader coach. I think we're both perfectionists. I'm not sure who rubbed off on whom. I think I have a bit of OCD for sure. We are both passionate about our career choices. She has certainly been instrumental and supportive of me reaching my career goals. She is one smart lady. Our dogs are our two young'uns. If they could talk, they would have some good stories."

I had an opportunity to talk with Maggie Jameson as she finished her school day at Abbeville High School one afternoon. She had recently returned from a trip to London where she accompanied four of her cheerleading squad. Maggie is the cheerleader coach, now in her second year of coaching varsity. During the opening of our conversation I told her that Benji Greeson and I had interviewed her grandfather, Coach Red Jameson at their home for the Abbeville Football book a few years prior. I asked how Red and Margaret, her grandparents, were doing. She said they were doing well, up in age but doing okay. Maggie was into her fourth year of teaching. She had been honored with Teacher of the Year in Abbeville in 2019. She was on her way to Myrtle Beach for a ceremony the first time Clay I had talked as he commuted to Charlotte. She added that it was not uncommon for them to often be often heading in opposite directions.

Clay and Maggie

Time to chat with Maggie Jamison: Maggie, give me your version of your first meeting with Clay.

> "I was best friends at the time with Clay's best friend's girlfriend. His drummer and my friend had been dating. To be honest, I don't really know what attracted me to Clay. He had a girlfriend at the time. We were probably having a little too much fun for our age. I'm not exactly sure how it happened. It just did."

Clay told me that you and he were both probably perfectionist. How do you make that work in your relationship?

> "We just argue all the time. I'm right, but we just agree that we're going to disagree on who is right. I helped manage his career for a while I was in college but not so much anymore."

Were you involved in the Idol experience?

Maggie acknowledged that she had traveled with him through the entire event, from his first trip in Atlanta through all the competition including the last stop in Hawaii.

> "The experience was good. It was highly organized. It was structured for what was expected of the contestants. Not that it is staged, but they do over direct. Everyone I met was extremely nice. I think, going into it, we had the perception that it might be all fake, but we were pleasantly surprised that it wasn't. All the Idol stories were real. They made it fit for the television audience."

Clay had mentioned attending one of the Abbeville High School football playoff games, the one where they were beaten and eliminated one game shy of competing for their potential fifth state title. How much of a letdown was it from a cheerleader coach's perspective?

> "It has been fun, Abbeville winning four consecutive state AA titles. I attended Ware Shoals High School. We were not good at football, so I had been accustomed to cheering

> for a losing team. Up until this year none of my girls had ever been part of a losing season. Abbeville had always won the state title. I had to teach them how to cope with a loss after they had always been cheering for a winner. It's tough to cheer when you're not on the winning side."

Maggie commutes to Abbeville from just across the Georgia line, about a 25-minute ride each school day. There she and Clay live in what he refers to as their tiny house.

> "Yeah, we live there. We used to live in the Fellowship Hall in Elberton. I like the tiny house much better. We just must be mindful of getting into each other's space. Clay often practices his guitar outside. We do our best to avoid crowding one another too much. I give him his space but support him. I knew going into this relationship that his previous girlfriend did not support his music even though he was crazy about her. He ended up putting his music on the backburner because of it. I knew from the get-go that music was first. He had told me that when we had first begun hanging out together. His music was first. I was second."

This caught me off guard, a woman accepting the second spot over anything. My wife certainly would not handle those circumstances very well, that is if I were stupid enough to say it. How do you deal with that pecking order?

> "I guess because I put my career first as well. We were intent on being successful before our relationship developed. I have never known anything different with Clay. Before we even began dating, we had that conversation. I understood his music came first. We were in high school and both had personal goals."

What are your thoughts on Clay's music and where it has gone up to this point?

> "He has been doing good. We always talk about where he is and where he needs to go, and he can be all over the place. He is at a spot now where he is doing almost

everything when it comes to his career. I used to do a lot for him. I have taken a step back to allow him the space to handle it on his own, but I am big on keeping him as humble as possible. We looked at management opportunities. There were two guys who had made offers. One of them we really liked. The other one was a bit too iffy, not sure if we could trust him to have Clay's best interest. Everything this one guy was offering to have Clay was already doing. This has probably been one of his biggest career hurtles, wondering what's the next stop. I believe Clay needs to be back in Nashville and let someone else handle his career. Clay is too hands-on though, always wanting to do it himself.

I feel like a few years ago when I was handling everything for him, he wasn't as hands-on because I was doing it for him. It might have been easier for him to give it to someone else. Now, that he has been doing it all, he's more reluctant to give it away."

Clay seemed excited during the holidays doing charity performances.

"He's going to be talking to kindergarteners again. He hated school but he likes this age group."

I laughed, telling Maggie that Clay credits her with helping him in school.

"I really didn't think he was going to graduate. I graduated at the top of my class so dating a boy that might not graduate seemed quite interesting to me. We spent at least four months trying to get him through math. I would do his math at home and then he would have to take his test."

Clay had talked about how good Jimmy Jones was in math and how he had been quite creative in his cheating techniques off Jimmy's test.

"Those two were horrible in school with their antics. If I had been their teacher, I would have had them kicked out of class. They strung fishing line through a science class. Did he tell you about that one? He could do this stuff and never get into any trouble for it. They never got sent from class or suspended. I would have suspended them in a heartbeat.

Clay is extremely focused when it comes to music. He is extremely focused, sometimes almost too much. When I get home from work that's all he wants to talk about. I must remind him that I had a good day too. I think it is because he is at home all day alone. When I get home, he wants to talk to me about everything he thought about during the day. I have been teaching 60 kids all day. I am not necessarily in the mood for hearing the 19 things he has been thinking about all day.

We have been together now going on nine years. We grew up together. Not necessarily our entire life though because I did go to college for four years, and we didn't attend the same high school. We were for the most part living together though. We did have to learn what aggravates each other and how to get around it."

I warned Clay that when I talked to Maggie, I was going to ask her about the marriage thing. How did she see it? Did they talk around it? Maggie did not blink and answered,

"He talks around it. He has always said that he needs to be successful before we get married. His level of success changes each time he meets his goal. Funny thing. I just don't talk about it anymore because it just frustrates me when we talk about it. He always talks around it. I think he associates being married with having kids. He is not ready to have kids. I have heard all kinds of excuses from that boy. I have heard he can't afford to buy me a ring now. I have heard that he must first be successful and able to provide.

Clay is old school in that way. When I graduated college, he didn't really want me to start working. He said that I could stay home. I told him he did not have to worry about that, me not staying home since we were not married. He talks around it, so I just don't bring it up anymore. I just don't get into that conversation. He is very shy and doesn't like talking about why he feels so strongly about this situation.

He has always been shy, but he has learned how to talk to people. I don't enjoy talking to people. If they don't talk to me first, I'm not worrying about it. I teach all the time but if kids do not want to talk to me, I'm not going to beg them to do it. Clay will look at me and question as to why I did not speak to a certain person. My come back is I cannot even think of that person's name, much less a reason to speak to them. Clay uses the 'hey man' greeting all the time, repeating himself twelve times. Everybody is his brother. He calls everyone brother. Everyone is either man or brother and I say, 'Clay'? He fusses sometimes saying I treat him like one of my students. I really try not to do that."

Digging for dirt, I asked Maggie for some of the funniest Clay stories, the outtakes and those from the blooper reel.

"There are so many things, I can't think of them right now. Funny. We have been together so long I guess we are an open book with family and friends. There are some things I cannot talk about, being a teacher in Abbeville. I do remember long ago, Clay having this party and we invited a bunch of our friends. He got so torn up that he asked me to call his mama. I told him; I am not calling your mama. You will die before I call your mama. Clay will get sick every time he drinks. I remind you; this was a long time ago, not recently. Jimmy Jones was there and those two would try to see who could get drunk the fastest. He had gotten so sick that night that he wanted me to call his mama. I told him I would take him to the hospital, but I wasn't calling his mama. He has always been a mama's boy. The first time his mama found out we were seeing one another she took away Clay's phone as punishment. She didn't warm up to me for a while but now everything is fine. She will even sometimes take my side over his.

> Clay and I have grown up a lot together. Seems in the last year though that we are always running in the opposite direction. Our careers keep us busy. We tend to stay in the road. I am nursing a black eye right now. One of my cheerleaders elbowed me in the eye. Yesterday my eye was swollen shut. I asked Clay if I could borrow a pair of his sunglasses to wear to a meeting. He said no, they'll think you got beaten up."

I warned Maggie that I might tell him that I heard about her making up the cheerleader story to cover for him being a woman beater. I didn't want Henry Green from Abbeville's Press and Banner newspaper to include an article about Clay's physical abuse. They say there is no such thing as bad PR. She knows Henry quite well too.

Maggie continues,

> "One thing that bothered us during Idol is that we couldn't go out to dinner or the grocery store. Someone would spot him. You had to think about the PR, or someone would want to conduct an interview. It was very awkward. I don't think his mama understood it until she was out with us one time and experienced it firsthand. People will stop and want to talk to you while you are trying to have your meal. You don't want to be rude and keep eating while they are just standing there. That was the learning curve from Idol; staying prepared for these situations when people recognized him. Local to national exposure changes the scenario.
>
> It's funny how everyone wants to be your friend after something like this. It makes you think; they weren't friends before but now they are wanting to be. Clay had never had to deal with this, so it was an adjustment. It's back to the music always comes first thing. I had gotten used to people stopping by and acknowledging themselves as fans. It makes it difficult to go out it in public because Clay is not the type to stay home all the time. When Clay is frustrated, he is not a fun person to be around. It makes him grumpy. Clay's mama says men are like that."

If you could sit Clay down right now, what advice would you give him on moving forward in his career and with your relationship?

"I think he needs to be back in Nashville instead of Elberton. I'm fine with him being back there. We did it for a year. He was home most weekends and we made it work. He needs to rekindle those relationships he made while there. If you want a publishing deal, those people are in Nashville. If you don't live in Nashville, some venues can be subject to paying you more to travel back and forth. I am not sure that is what Clay wants to do right now.

Clay struggles with what he wants to do, perform, or write music. I had to decide from a teaching perspective. I knew I wanted to teach but I had to decide what subject I wanted to teach. Being a songwriter is entirely different from being an artist. He needs to choose one and pursue it. I don't think he can decide which one for him. I really don't care which one so long as he is happy with the choices he makes.

I think he fears he is going to miss out on something, regret something ten years down the road. You must be confident with whatever you are doing. Same goes for choosing the manager contract. Just be okay with what you decide. It seems to me that many of the artists were songwriters first and the publishing companies helped them get their record deals. The real money comes from songwriting. By the time you become a recording artist, there are so many people along that are needed to be part of it. They get their piece of it and much time is spent touring.

He has developed many contacts that he has cowritten with and talked with a couple of publishers. Sometimes I think he tends to scare them off because he isn't sure what he really wants to do. My spin is to go into it confident that yes, I want a publishing deal. I might not want one with you but, yes, I want a publishing deal. You never know how things work, some moving from one publishing house to another. Keep your options open. Like in teaching, I might not know who I am working with right now that might help me in the future, so you must be able to nurture these situations, especially with the Nashville folks.

Locally, Clay does a wonderful job contacting places because he likes the people who run them. I don't think he is able to transfer that to Nashville and make it work. I think the right management could definitely help. We argued this fact about him needing management, but we didn't think the options presenting themselves were the best ones at the time. Much of what was in the contracts was just too vague. We felt that they were not being specific enough and it could be interpreted differently.

Clay is the type that every little detail needs to be spelled out. Sometimes being too specific helps but it can also hurt. Clay listens to advice but then tends to argue why his way is the better option. I think he wants to bounce his ideas and then have us argue his ideas for him. My take is why are you even asking me if you have basically already made your mind up. No need to argue if your mind has already been made up.

Clay will be in Nashville for a week in February. Unfortunately, a lot of times in Nashville you don't get paid for playing. That makes it tough to have band members because they don't want to play free. When Clay was there for the year, that was the second time he had been to Nashville. When we graduated high school, he had decided to go to Nashville. I was going to enroll at Belmont, one of the Nashville schools. I sent in an application and he had gotten a job lined up. Then he decided he wasn't going to do that. He ended up staying in Elberton making me look dumb for sending in a college application.

The second time, he ended up going in October I was already in a year contract teaching, so I stayed here. We were paying two rents. I did move to Nashville for the summer with him when it was time for me to think about a new contract. Sadly, he could not decide what he wanted to do so I committed to a contract at home. I think he might have stayed if I had been there to help. He is a homebody which is not necessarily a bad thing. Clay does love to travel as well but he does not like to stay away from home too long. I love to travel too."

I commented that the two dogs appear to be their babies.

"Yes, they are. Clay used them on the cover of his new album. All my friends teased me about the dogs making the album cover and I didn't. I said yeah. I know. That always happens."

What about Uncle Norman?

"Norman was a trip. He was incredibly old school. He grew up in that generation and you never knew what he might say. Norman was instrumental in getting him started playing music. Norman was always there and fostering that relationship. Clay was with him when he died. That was tough on him. He had been sick, but he had not been deathly sick. It caught everyone by surprise. Clay called me and asked me to contact his mama in Athens. I arrived right after Norman passed. Clay was a mess because he was so close to Norman. I always brought Norman food from my mama's. He loved her cooking. He always treated me nice."

We finished the phone interview while Maggie was driving home from Abbeville. It was a déjà vu moment. The first conversation that Clay and I had had was during his drive to Charlotte. On a somber note, Maggie's grandfather passed sometime shortly after our conversation. How untimely after we had just been talking about Coach Jameson.

Coach Robert B. 'Red' Jameson
March 9, 1931 – February 16, 2020

Somewhere Down the Road

This segment was conducted a week after Maggie and Clay celebrated the life of her departed grandfather. Maggie, according to Clay, was doing as well as could be expected given the circumstances of such a loss. Prayer warriors maintained a vigilant awareness for her and her family. The coach will certainly be missed by family and friends.

Winding down the process of telling his story, Clay continues to focus on what might be ahead. Januarys are typically slow months according to him. This is more of a rebooting process and laying the groundwork for the challenges and opportunities ahead. The life of self employment in any occupation keeps one on their toes if they are diligent in maintaining and expanding a business regardless of the path chosen. The music industry is no different. Clay is not one to sit idly on the sidelines waiting for opportunities to come to him. Winter months can often be slow, but this is the time to prepare for a new season. Like a farmer preparing their land for the upcoming planting season, Clay must till the ground in preparation for a new seed to be sown in his music career. The tools of the trade might be different, but preparation is preparation.

Right now, Clay finds himself 'Somewhere In Between' where he has been and where he is heading, life hinging on the path best chosen. There will always be forks in the roads. Choosing the best route is of the utmost importance to maintain the momentum and minimize the obstacles that might hamper the journey. Big pictures are inspired by equally large dreams and goals. Staying focused is of the utmost importance. Fending off discouragement and frustration can be a constant battle. Clay remains positive and upbeat. His chosen direction and its ultimate ending are in God's hands. His faith remains strong. If it is meant to be it will happen on His timetable, not Clays. All Clay can do is nudge it along as best he can and pray it all works out in the end.

Clay explains where he is,

> "The last few weeks have been phone calls and emails. To assist in keeping me on track I am now using a day planner calendar to track my week, what I have accomplished, and where I have missed opportunities. It is extremely easy being self-employed, to drift off track what needs to be done and what you should be doing. Having this tool on my desk has been extremely beneficial as 2020 rolls out. I have taken the old fashion approach for maintaining my schedule. I still utilize my phone, but this technique is in my face every day. It seems to be helping me. I track my Mondays through Saturdays on the planner.
>
> The visibility of the planner on my desk has stimulated my motivation. By week's end I can see right there what I have accomplished or if I have wasted time. The last thing I want to see is too many days of empty entries. This at least tells me that I have been doing my best to make contacts, send emails, and do what I need to do to keep everything moving in 2020. This tool has made me more successful than usual this time of year.
>
> So far, I am averaging upwards of thirty emails and phone calls weekly, contacting new and old venues. With this comes an emotional roller-coaster ride. Some responses indicate that the venues would love to book me, but their schedules are full. Some don't respond at all or immediately. Then days later I might hear back from some of them. This does not help my morale when I'm sitting on ready and willing to work. On average I receive about 25% response to those I send. All of these do not pan out though. Unfortunately, those on the booking end do not comprehend the importance of the feedback or the urgency to respond. Singers, artists have bills just like anyone. Remaining gainfully employed helps pay those bills. Only receiving 25% response, good or bad, does not meet my expectations.
>
> On the flipside, I have venues that contact me. Most of the time these are ones I have been working. This does not

open me up to new markets where much of my focus will be in 2020. Many of the emails and phone calls are pursuing the new markets rather than those I have already established. As I have disclosed, I'm trying to expand beyond Georgia, South and North Carolina. That does not mean that I'm not thankful and blessed to have the local markets. At the end of the day, it is all about growing my brand, exposure to areas that have never heard of Clay Page."

If you had a wish list, how many dates would you be satisfied with booking monthly?

"Honestly, my dream is to work once weekly, maybe the weekend, if these were ticketed events. My goals have changed frequently."

I interrupted Clay, telling him that Maggie had validated that point, his goals constantly changing.

"At the end of the day, is this not what entertainers are supposed to be pursuing. Change and growth go hand in hand. Ten years ago, I made a goal that if I could just play music for a living I would be satisfied. I met that goal. I've been living that dream."

Have you completely discounted seeking management for your career?

"I've marked this off my current list. I have nothing against those I have talked with and mean no disrespect. At some point I may be more open to this. I am just not currently ready for that type of relationship in my career. I am satisfied with my choice of being the one man show. Handling the promotions, marketing, booking, songwriting, and social media content. I have shot two music videos in the past month. One dear friend in Greenwood shot one for me, gifted it somewhat.

Momentum from the American Idol exposure has been on the decline. To fill this void, I am anticipating an upswing

> in my following once I release these videos. I am hopeful they will stimulate more engagements. It is back to my new planner. Not one to look back on that calendar on Friday and Saturday and realize I fell short on optimizing my week. This drives me crazy, being unproductive or wasting valuable time. When it's behind you, you cannot go backwards. It defeats the purpose of having goals."

I told Clay that I had asked Maggie during our chat if she had any advice to give him, what advice would she give him concerning the direction of his career. Hers was simply encourage him to return to Nashville. Her spin had been that Clay had developed plenty of contacts while there and cowriting opportunities. The breakthrough moment would happen in Nashville.

Clay thought on this and then responded.

> "That may very well be the case. It has crossed my mind. Being home has been great, but I have learned something about myself. There is beauty in missing home too. After I have been on the road, there is nothing better than the feeling of returning home. It is always a constant struggle for me, not really wanting to leave home. When I am out on the road, I am always missing home. For some reason flying makes these feelings worse than when I am driving. There is just no better feeling after having been gone for any period, driving down the road toward home. I have learned I almost get a high from that. That said, I want to get out and play knowing at the end, I'm heading back. That makes me happy."

It was time for me to flip it on Clay. I reminded him that he had all these goals about breaking into new markets. If any of these fell into place, he would be away from home, maybe for extended periods. Was he prepared, given what he had just shared?

> "That's just it. Back to the manager decision. I met with a lawyer in Nashville recently. My grandmother accompanied me. This was an enjoyable experience, talking with the lawyer. He put a spin on it that put things in perspective for me. He said, 'Managers work for you.

When you sign a record or publishing deal, you work for them.' When I lived in Nashville, I had some great mentors. I met with them regularly while there. Since moving back home, I have not kept in touch with them and haven't had mentors here to direct me in my career. Meeting with the lawyer reminded me of being in a mentoring session. He helped me focus and calibrate where I am in my career.

He told me that if I am playing Georgia, South Carolina, North Carolina, and Alabama I was in a great region. He reminded me that I was just a few hours away from several major markets. He suggested that I make the most of my business and focus on those markets. Building and growing in those markets was crucial and growing in the newer markets was a smaller percentage. There is nothing wrong with going to California or Texas and possibly losing money considering the expenses required. However, I must keep it in perspective that the exposure might be worth it. I left Nashville, a new fire lit and closed the management deal door."

I hit Clay with what I considered to be the important question. Was his goal for 2020 to be a performing artist or a published songwriter? My spin, choose one ahead of the other, make it the top priority and focus on it first.

"Gees, that's a tough one you're tossing at me."

I told Clay it shouldn't be. Prioritizing is always critical in any job, career, or life in general. Without picking one as the primary focus, how do you keep the train on the tracks? One man's opinion, I posed the question, which one did he feel the most important in 2020, songwriter or performer. Of course, to add a little extra drama, I hummed the Jeopardy theme song, one minute for your answer.

Laughing Clay responded,

> "I would probably have to say performer. I can go without writing a song for weeks…"

Suddenly the phone went dead in mid-sentence. I was thinking this was a unique way for him to weenie out of a response. Eventually we restored the phone connection.

> "I can go without writing a song, but I cannot go two or three days without playing my guitar."

I reiterated that this was not the question. He was taking the politician's approach by not answering what I had asked. I clarified that I did not mean writing a song. My question was simple. Was it his goal to be a singer-performer or to have his songs published?

> "I would still say performer. With my current goals, this aligns with where I am for 2020. Besides career goals, I have plenty of personal goals as well."

Our conversation along these lines continued. I recanted that I once sent him a text along these lines and feared maybe I had insulted him with my suggestion. In the text I had asked Clay if he had ever considered approaching someone like Laine Hardy, the American Idol winner, to inquire if he might record one of his songs. What do I know other than having stayed in a Holliday Inn Express a few times?

> "That is a great question. Using Laine for example. He and I sing different styles of music. I'm more of a 90s, Alan Jackson, Dwight Yokam, Allman Brothers style. I feel he is more of a Delta, Louisiana, swamp country genre. I mean nothing disrespectful from that description. My leaning is to performing right now. I own the rights to my songs, and they are published through BMI.
>
> Speaking of goals, one of my goals in 2020 is to consolidate some of my debt. I make money playing shows. Much of my income is generated from these performances. Live shows are my livelihood. That poses a dilemma

though, balancing playing live shows and not hurting the Clay Page brand while keeping me moving in the right direction. Knocking down debt is a primary focus. Like anything, success doesn't come cheap. Those two music videos if marketed properly should boost my career as promotions and more exposure. It's a necessity to continue promoting songs and keep them relevant to the public. Doing so re-sparks the songs. I research my songs to determine which ones are popular. This leads to doing the videos, cashing in on their popularity.

I am not shy about working. I have mentioned that my granddaddy instilled some work ethics in me. I helped him with his pressure washing before he passed away. I learned that one can never be too humble to do what it necessary to pay the bills.

To keep the interest and diversity, I now offer three packages. One is a popup show. The second is a base pay show. The third is a ticketed event. Working or not working, bills must be paid. That's where I must be creative in ways to generate revenue. I have a single recorded that I have not released yet but it is scheduled for a May release. Spring and summer will be an active time for new material. I'm back full circle. Being an artist generates income. One thing for sure, no one is going to work your garden as hard as the person planting the garden. That just so happens to be me, the gardener.

I have the capability of recording music here at my tiny house, but the quality might not be the best to use for a release. I have raised that bar professionally through the studio recordings in Nashville. Recording here would be going backwards and probably foolish. My equipment might suffice in producing something that can be pitched to film to be used in a fifteen second jingle. Film is just another potential avenue for me to utilize my talent. From a publishing standpoint I might be able to utilize for film opportunities. It might consist of acoustical guitar and a brief vocal track. Revenue can be generated through sink play and film usage. This is just another option, where I am as I venture into 2020.

I have been focused on identifying my strengths as well as my weaknesses as a musician and in my personal life. Just what is Clay Page good at. Before I moved to Nashville, I had a pressure washer business here. I learned from Papa Ricky when his health was failing, to help him on some of his pressure washing jobs. By doing this, I learned from the best. Work is work and you must be willing to do what you must do to fill the slow times.

I'm heading back to Nashville for a week. I have several venues booked, including the National Turkey Federation Convention. Five appearances there and they are all for promotions. I am not being paid to appear at any of them. To offset some of my expenses for that trip, I have gotten a bit creative. I reached out to some outfitters, those that make turkey calls, hunting apparel, and even one that has a hunting experience on a plantation in Georgia. With these five shows in Nashville, it would be the perfect scenario for sponsorship. I can represent their brands during the appearances and through my social media sites. This might include meet and greets at their booths. Like the saying goes, failing is not an option. There's money to be made if you are willing to work and be creative.

I have the Abbeville Opera House performance slated for the end of February. This is a ticketed event. With that comes sacrifices. I must be cautious not to overbook the local areas leading into this date so that I don't adversely impact potential attendance. A sellout would be exceptional for my resume. Ticket sales enhance the brand. Hopefully, by the end of 2020, attendance numbers and my social media following will indicate growth in my brand.

I know I'm not the most talented out there. There are people singing in their bedrooms that can blow me out of the water. You have got to want your goals and your dreams. Traveling this road, you gain experience and knowledge along the way if you are patient and do your homework. I feel sometimes that I understand more about the business that I should know at the level I am currently at if that makes any sense. This can be a good thing. People are always trying to sway me one way or the other, pursue a publishing deal or don't pursue a publishing deal. I admire singer-songwriter Toby Keith. From what I read, he did it the right way, holding onto his publishing and taking ownership of his career.

I am certainly not professing that I have everything figured out. Obviously, if I did, I be at a better place. I passionately believe that there will be that day soon when all my hard work is going to pay off. The struggles I have endured will equate to something great. When that day arrives, it will make everything that I have gone through worthwhile. It can seem confusing at times but every day I learn something about the music business, good or bad. It might seem that my career is all over the place, but I try to make the best decisions, those that will hopefully pay off eventually. I continue to be blessed, no matter where it ends. I am without a doubt living my dream. What else can be said? So many never follow their dream and have regrets. I thank those who have made it possible for me to be where I am now and for those who support me as I continue in my quest. Somewhere down the road it will all work out, whether it is Clay Page the artist working certain avenues, Clay Page the publisher working other avenues, or Clay Page the songwriter still writing music for himself or others."

Clay continues to be 'Somewhere In Between' in his pursuit of the American Dream. No doubt he is in it for the long haul, too much time and money invested to turn back now. Is Clay where he wants to be at this snapshot in time? Certainly not. Has he achieved many of his goals? Absolutely. Does he aspire to soar even higher? With no doubt. Yes, short term goals constantly change, often flip flopping back and forth. Ultimately, Clay remains focused and grounded. He is a Georgia country boy, proud of his roots and humble surroundings. Testimony to his convictions, he has driven that Isuzu Rodeo with 300,000 plus road miles on it, continues to live in his 480 square foot tiny house with Maggie, and loves nothing better than being home, or at least heading in a homeward direction after a road trip. If you think about it, is this not the persona of the real deal country singer?

Clay is as genuine as they come, from his boyish looks to his infectious smile. With Clay, there is no put on. He often depicts himself as unpolished and a tad introverted in some circumstances when it comes to meeting people and speaking in front of a crowd. The shyness and uncertainty vanish though when he picks up his guitar. Is he a powerhouse singer with booming vocals? Clay admits he is not. His guitar playing does his talking for him, leaving no doubt he is a talented force to be reckoned with. Focused and determined, there is no telling where this young man will end up. Performing artist or accomplished songwriter, he will succeed no matter which path he chooses. David Jones inspired him. Uncle Norman saw his potential. Clay's parents ensured he followed his dream. Vernon Brown helped him develop his skills. Maggie continues to support Clay wherever his career takes him. One thing for sure, while this chapter ends, there are many more pages to be written in Clay Page's journey.

Southern Fried Morning Show

I had the opportunity to chat with our mutual friend, Benji Greeson, host of Abbeville's WZLA 92.9 Southern Fried Morning Show. He shared how he and Clay had met and his friendship with the young entertainer.

"We first met through the morning show. I'll go online and browse social media. People post videos of them singing and if they are good, I will sometimes toss out an invite to join me on the show. I did that with Clay close to six years ago. I met him within the first year that we started the Morning Show. He was probably no more than eighteen or nineteen years old then. He and another guy showed up and sang a couple of songs. Back then, he was just going out and gigging, playing here and there. People knew of him, but he had not really blown up yet.

We continued to keep in touch. It was probably nearly a year later that he came back on the show. I remember his second appearance more than his first because I noticed how his writing and performance had almost tripled from where it had been. He was an unbelievable performer. We stayed in touch. I would try to go where he was performing and check him out. Three or four more appearances on the show and he became kind of a regular. We started calling him Cousin Clay. He would come in and sit down, was so likable and laid back. He fit in well with our format.

Fast forward to the start of the American Idol thing. I had seen a posting he had online of him and the Hollywood Hills sign. I asked him the next time he came into the studio about it, thinking he had gone to Los Angeles to sign a record deal. He told me that he had some big things cooking but he could not talk about them yet. He said he really wanted to tell me, but I would know about his little secret pretty soon. That was the beginning of American Idol. He had already completed his audition in Atlanta, his Idaho audition in front of the judges and had finished the Hollywood rounds in LA.

Oddly, it had gone from me texting him to come on the show to him texting me and saying he could basically do nothing himself. Everything had to be booked through an American Idol publicist. He said that it was very weird and not something he was accustomed to doing. While he was on Idol he was under contract and whatever he did they had to approve of everything. He could not book anything or talk to anyone without their permission. There for a couple of months it was handled exclusively by them. Idol was good about setting it up because it was essentially his home base area.

We were able to set up three or four interviews during his time on Idol. Usually he would be promoting Idol or the show's episode. What was really funny was he was filling up bars and clubs before, but he then went to being worldwide famous after appearing on Idol. On social media you would see people popping up from places like Scotland or France. He went from being a local celebrity to people knowing his name nationwide. That was wild.

People think it was an overnight thing for Clay, but he had been working this and playing for years. Since he was about sixteen or so, long before he landed the American Idol deal. When that finally ended and he wasn't under their thumb, he appeared on the show and we would talk about his journey. If he is in town and we're both free, we'll meet for lunch. I really saw where his career was headed. We would go do lunch at the Rough House on the Abbeville square. We would not be able to eat because people would recognize him. They would want to talk to him or take photos with him or get his autograph. A 30-minute lunch would be more like an hour or longer. Every other person that came through the door would immediately come over to our table."

Benji, at that point, did you ever consider it might be a good idea to offer to be his agent and manager?

Laughing, Benji said,

> "We had always just clicked and had a good time together. When he moved to Nashville, he recorded the Southbound album. After he recorded it, he returned home and wanted to have his record release party in his hometown, Elberton. Just so happens the date he chose was his birthday. He asked if I would MC the show for him. This was before American Idol. That was the first night that I realized just how incredible Clay was. The venue seated 350 seats and there was not an empty seat in the house. I got up there and introduced a couple of opening acts. Then he and I did something like what we did at the Abbeville Opera House appearance. We sat on stage and discussed Nashville and the people he had met while there like David Lee Murphy.
>
> Move on to now when we had the Clay Page and Friends event at the Opera House. Again, there were 300 or so people packed in there as well. He has some star power to him. He is very charismatic. He is a regular guy and does well at being a singer-songwriter. He plays this up well, signing the kids' stuff."

Do you have any dirt on Clay, rare outtakes, blooper moments, something funny or out of the ordinary while with him?

> "I can't say I know any dirt on him. He is just a normal, regular guy. We have not run into any debauchery yet. It is not really dirt, but it was kind of funny at the Opera House. I ventured backstage while the openers were performing. Clay and several of his band were back there, a guitar player, a drummer named Cody. Cody did not have his box drum backstage and they were trying to warm up a bit. He asked me to hold this pizza box. I looked at him, like what? He said he had a couple of coat hangers and he wanted me to be his drum, to hold the pizza box in place. He used the coat hangers and pizza box to warm up in the dressing room. I was the drum stand."

If you could sit Clay down in front of you, what advice would you, the worldly guy, give him?

> "Keep doing what he is doing. Continue to be humble, nice, and as regular person. If you would want someone to be a role model, Clay would be the person to put in that role. He just likes hunting, fishing, hanging out, and playing country music. He's a normal regular guy with a career path steadily pointing upwards. I don't have any advice as far as that goes. He is crossing all the T's and dotting all the I's. He loves his family. He is an animal lover. He dearly loves his dogs. I was talking to him recently and he told me that hunting had become kind of hard. He said his heart just doesn't want to venture out there and kill anything. Unless he knows it's going on the plate or in the freezer, he doesn't want to pull the trigger on anything."

What do you think about Clay maybe going back to Nashville? Several people close to him have indicated that it might not be a bad idea.

> "Self-promotion is hard. Staying on social media, doing your own promoting, and booking is a full-time job. I'm not sure what Clay personally wants out of this. Is he satisfied where he is now or if he wants to be on an arena tour 200 days a year? He has the talent to do whatever he wants to do. It depends on where he wants to go with it. Having a manager is a tough decision. Turning it over to someone you think you can trust. You never know whether they are just out to make a dollar or are out to get you. Once you sign ownership over to them, are they going to look out for you or just file the paperwork away and forget about you, owning you forever. It is a scary thing. I think the Lord already knows the right path for him and right thing will come along and will be beneficial to him and his career.
>
> You must be really carful when in a place like Nashville. There are so many just waiting to capitalize and own your rights. It is a business and can be a shady business as well. I think Clay possesses a natural precautionary ability and it is

warranted. One bad move and you are done. It is scary, especially if you're counting on it for your career, your livelihood. Knowing Clay, he'll do just fine."

Benji with Clay at the Radio Station

Historical Ramifications

The Tour That Never Happened

Life is often filled with unexpected surprises. Some good. Some not so good. Clay, like most people, could never have envisioned the scenario that would drastically alter the world. Something historical and quite horrific was unleashed with origins traced back to China. It was almost on an apocalyptic scale while others referenced its impact to something of biblical proportions. The beast had no face. It was invisible but it had a name, Covid-19 or commonly called the coronavirus. It would impact the world epically, inflicting illness, death, and crashing a prosperous economy. Social distancing would become the new dreaded catch phrase. With its arrival the nation came to a crashing standstill.

States, cities, businesses, churches were ordered closed by the government. The scientific and medical community suggested that the world's population confine themselves to their homes, wash their hands constantly, wear masks, and practice social distancing of at least six feet. Avoid touching your face with your hands, especially your mouth, nose, and eyes. People were dying by the thousands. Some argued that the counts were exaggerated while others practiced fear mongering. Eventually the horror and terror caused by an invisible foe turned sadly political.

People struggled to understand why big box stores could remain open but small businesses and even churches were ordered closed. The argument of essential versus nonessential made no sense to most as if a virus could know the difference between the two. Liquor stores were considered essential while hair salons, barbershops and churches were not. The method to this unfolding madness made absolutely no sense. Millions of people found themselves with no jobs, no income and confined to their homes. Ironically, most complied with this suggested behavior. The abnormally new normal had begun.

Clay Page found himself in the middle of this historical moment, one that he would rather have had no part in experiencing. He, as most, had landed on the nonessential side of the fence. Government had somehow designated those essential and those not. His livelihood evaporated in a blink. With no venues, no bars, no festivals what was he supposed to do with this madhouse on steroids and a world coming to a screeching stop? Clay puts his spin on it and how it impacted his life.

No one could have prepared us for the events that would come crashing down on us during this book project. Clay had huge plans for traveling across this great nation to perform at numerous venues along the way, but plans do not always work out as envisioned. The world came under attack by an invisible foe, one unleashed in China and soon spread like nothing ever before. We became familiar with the term, Coronavirus. Social activity came to a standstill to minimize the spread of this deadly disease.

Professional sports worldwide came to a screeching halt. All activities placing people in close proximity were no more. Federal, state and/or local governments began ordering the closures of restaurants for dinning in and bars had to close their doors to business. Movie theaters, bowling alleys, parks, beaches, all entertainment venues were ordered to shudder their doors. Only venues considered essential were allowed to function. Social distancing became the new normal. Stay at home except when buying groceries, visiting pharmacies or doctors was advised. Some states even mandated a stay at home policy.

Millions of people could no longer report to work or had no place to go because the businesses were no longer operational. Clay Page's livelihood was impacted as well. There were no longer any venues operating that cater to entertainment of any kind. Being neighborly and doing the right thing like visiting Vet centers, nursing facilities, or schools were presently a thing of the past.

Clay faced adversity like nothing that had ever challenged him. Well laid plans of a cross country tour went up in smoke. His vision of 2020 became a cloudy blur. The singer-songwriter now faced something unimaginable. Question. Can a country boy really survive? Time to hear it from Clay's perspective; a bonus chapter that pays no dividends. Just when we thought the story was a wrap, here we are, part of the wrong side of history. Take it away Clay.

> "I was preparing for my tour when Covid-19 blew it up. Normally April through around August is my busiest time of the year. From a financial perspective this time period is usually filled with opportunities for me to bank some money. My plan for spring and summer is usually developed three months prior. I had devoted much time planning ticketed events for 2020. With the arrival of Covid the domino effect began. My month-long tour for April vanished in a puff of smoke.
>
> At first my April trek was going to be at best a break-even experience, but that was okay because I looked for it to be a

promotion of my brand. Ironically, it evolved into a tour where I was going to pocket some money instead. I planned to get a rental car in Elberton for the trip to the West Coast.'

Hold it. I had to interrupt and stop Clay here. I could not believe it. Clay was not taking the legend, the Isuzu Rodeo with over 300,000 logged miles.

"No sir. I love living on the edge, but my folks told me that I was not going to that. I told them that's what makes it fun, not knowing whether you will make it there and back. This earthshattering event hit me hard personally. I found myself going through stages. It was tough to digest that the events I had spent months coordinating were now being canceled. Not only did I spend three months putting this together, I had spent my musical career waiting for such an eventful opportunity happening during the summer. Last year I did not have a chance to coordinate something on this scale because my time was devoted to Idol. Now with that behind me, my goal this year was to work harder than ever to promote the brand."

Walk the readers through the gambit of emotions you endured when reality slammed you between the eyes that this golden opportunity had gone up in smoke.

"The first week it hit me that it might not work I was extremely busy recording with a buddy of mine, Reggie Starrett. This kept my mind off it. I was thinking Covid-19, whatever. I just thought it was something being hyped by the media. I did not take it very seriously. The second week I thought maybe this thing was for real. I had my first cancellations from my planned tour. I remained in denial though thinking it would blow over. I was hesitant to call any of the other venues on the tour, believing if I did not contact them the events would happen as scheduled.

Week three they canceled the music festival, my biggest summer event of the year. This was the Southbound Music Festival in Elberton. It was in its second year. Various singers had submitted videos in a contest and winners by popular vote had been selected to perform on stage as well. This was going to be my biggest event of the year, a ticketed show. I had prepared for this one by not playing many venues locally so that I would not saturate the market going into it and adversely impact potential ticket sales. I turned down plenty of work since American Idol last year building up to this one show. Me, taking this approach does not make good financial sense to most, but from a career standpoint, it is the right choice for me. Financially speaking now, it did sort of bite me in the butt with the cancelation. You cannot foresee something like this happening unfortunately. You cannot plan for the contingency of a worldwide pandemic.

With that cancelation so far in advance, I realized that this virus pandemic was getting serious. I had pre-sold a few tickets for the Music Festival. In my line of work, I might often be living off the income of a show that has not happened yet. Now I was faced with refunding those tickets. It was not being rescheduled for a later date. It was canceled for this year. It's a big deal having large sponsors committed to it so far in advance. You cannot just drop it and then plan it again. I had never been faced with this challenge, refunding from the presales I no longer had. With growth comes growing pains. We did manage to refund all monies. It hit me hard just how real this was becoming. People might not realize it but there are not many sponsors spending marketing money right now in these uncertain and scary times. Think about it. Venues like radio might have a tough time selling commercial time to businesses that are closed. And closed for who knows how long.

I found myself going through the gambit of mood swings. I was mad. I was angry. I hit a slow spot. One weekend I probably indulged a little more than I normally do just so frustrated with the situation and how it was impacting my life. It got me down because I had been working so hard on this for three months. I just found myself mad and pissed off. I finally came to the realization after talking with others that I was not the only one going through this. I had to get beyond that poor me, feeling sorry for myself, phase. I began to wake up and see the whole country suffering. It was not just one man's burden.

I refocused my energy, connecting with my fans on social media. I began doing virtual shows. This did not happen immediately though. I spent at least a week without going on social media while I reassessed the situation and worked through a path moving forward. It was tough. I was literally 'somewhere in between' until I found my bearings again. I was at a low point, in a funk, but I came out of it and stopped feeling sorry for myself. I understood it. We were in this together…me and the whole country. Throughout plenty of people were reaching out to me. That adage that God works in mysterious ways had never spoken louder to me than at this time when I needed Him the most. It hit me that maybe just was God's plan, a way to get us to slow down and see the beauty in life, to quit worrying about the hustling and embrace what you have taken for granted.

No denying it, I had to go through the cycle, being in a funk, and worrying about what I was going to do with my music and my career. I had to reboot and explore a new mindset. The virtual tours and all possible avenues to generate income. I did The Square On Air Show with host Benji Greeson. It streamed live and was available worldwide. That gave me something to look forward to. It hit me that maybe this was what I was supposed to be doing. Benji had asked me to do it, but I had no idea that I would be the first guess on his very first episode airing on Sundays at 6 PM. It felt epic, appearing with my buddy Benji.

With Square On Air and cranking up my virtual tours and other media promotions, I climbed from the funk and started channeling my energy more positively. I was determined to make this work through these troubling and challenging times. I began working my website and began uploading my new merchandise including my new hats.

I have seen the hats on your website. Explain the significance of the two sets of numbers that are on the hats.

> "The '706' is the northeast Georgia area code. Those are the first three digits that appear on my phone number. The '864' numbers are the area code from maybe Calhoun Falls through Greenville, South Carolina. I came up with the idea after seeing area codes on merchandise when I lived in Nashville. It made sense to utilize the concept to connect with my Georgia-South Carolina fanbase. The '706' and '864' is 'Somewhere In Between' the two states. It might evolve into a song, a new promotion or even a financial plan someday. I have always had a creative mind. When my mind is not being creative, I get bored and that in turn bring s me down. I must constantly be busy, thinking, and doing something to stay satisfied."

With schools being closed and Maggie being impacted as well, just how has that affected your lives? You are both obviously at home and living in the confines of the tiny house 24/7. That must come with a few challenges. And, of course, your family lives there as well. You have been a close nit family. How about now? I have noticed by your posts on FB that you have reconnected with your fishing roots, something you mentioned you wanted to do more this year. Like magic. There you are.

> "In between that week of working video projects and that time of denial, I spent a week fishing. Returning to the lake life and fishing was great. I also hooked up with an old buddy of mine from school, Bentavious Allen. He was always a cool dude in school. There were times I was picked on and bullied during middle school, and he always had my back. I am glad I had a chance to reconnect with him. I have had to learn how to apply the brakes and just slow down.
>
> Through this I have aged a year celebrating my 26th birthday. I have learned to put it in perspective. I thought music was my life but there is more to life that just the grind and hustle. I have learned to balance it a bit. Still not the best but I am trying. With Maggie being home from

work we probably were about ready to kill one another the first couple of weeks. With a little over 400 square feet we had to adjust. I think with her being with me here, in my world, it has given her a better understanding of how I feel being at home waiting for her to come home from work each day. What I mean by this is that when she arrives, I have been here all day, emailing and working promotions, and then I am ready to go somewhere when she gets home. She has been away from home all day and is ready to stay home. Now, we are both ready to get out of here. She has the summer off from teaching, but we are usually on the road during much of that time while I'm playing shows. The last couple of years we have been on the go. Idol for example.

If anything, good has come out of this, I have learned to manage my finances better. We cannot dine out with everything basically closed. We have learned to eat at the house more like everyone else. Eating out is probably one of our largest expenses. Eating out is my hobby. I genuinely enjoy good food and don't mind paying for a quality meal. We both enjoy sushi. I love a good steak too. If eating can be a hobby, I guess it is ours."

Can either one of you cook?

"Maggie cooks. I have learned a few recipes through this home confinement. This might be a spin off…Clay Page's recipe book. I have learned to cook a venison burger over the past few weeks. It is my version of a garlic chipotle burger cooked on the backyard grill. I also have cooked lemon-teriyaki chicken wings. This is something I had never attempted. It's that being creative thing and trying to keep my mind occupied. Maggie is an excellent cook.

With all that fishing I have been doing, I got to check my country boy box to validate that I still can. We have fish in the freezer now. If we run out of food from the grocery we can survive on fish."

Does this mean you will be having a country boy's version of sushi…bass, brim, catfish, and crappie sushi?

> "I don't know if I could eat any of those raw. We only fry them. I used to hate sushi. Maggie turned me on to eating it. Sushi is for sure an acquired taste. As for my family we are closer if that is possible to be closer than we already were. It has opened my eyes up about a lot of things."

Have you seen your grandmother Camilla during this?

> "I have. I visited her a couple of times. I am a little hesitant though because I don't want to be the one that endangers that side of the family. The rest of us live here on the lake."

Where are you with everything right now?

> "I haven't been trying to book any new shows right now. It was such a kick in the gut losing those others, so I have been taking it slow. I'm not ready to put in three more months of work until I am confident that we have blue skies and coast is clear.
>
> I genuinely believe I have already had this virus. If I did not have Covid three or four months ago I had the respiratory flu. I never got tested for the flu, but the doctor told me I had the flu and it later turned into bronchitis. I had it two weeks straight while Maggie was in London with her cheerleaders. I credit her not getting it because I already had it while she was gone. Maybe I built up the immunity and could no longer transmit it. I suffered with bouts of being unable to breathe. There were a couple of times it scared me. I got out of bed unable to breathe with my heart rate elevated. I was freaking out and afraid. This would have been before anyone was talking about the virus. I had played in Charleston with a buddy of mine. I performed at a brewing company and visited the local VA there near the end of December. I might have contracted it then.
>
> There was a friend from Calhoun Falls that had traveled to Charleston to hear me play. He sent me a message a few weeks ago saying that he and I both had contracted Covid-19 at that time. He had gotten sick the same time as I did. His had been all respiratory related. I don't know if needles are involved in the testing, but I am afraid of them. I might consider being tested if they aren't to see if I had already had it. I pass out at the sight of a needle, plus I do not want to go near a doctor's office right now. I think there might have been more people in the area that had it early. Either Covid-19 had arrived in the Elberton area or a bad case of

the flu was wreaking havoc on the community. People were being tested for the flu with the results coming back negative. Doctors didn't know at that time to test for something else like Covid-19.

Maybe it was. Maybe it wasn't. I haven't been as concerned about it, leaning toward thinking it had been though. I think I had it. I wash my hands regularly and try to follow the other protocol that they recommend. I go back to God having a plan. Whatever happens…happens. I just keep the faith."

Where do you see the light at the end of your personal tunnel, or do you see that light yet?

"Elberton has begun opening things back up. The gym has opened. Some might think I am an idiot, but I have been going to the gym the past two weeks. They have beefed up their protocol as well, requiring more cleaning of the equipment. They have brought in more cleaning materials.

I just turned 26 and I am faced with more big decisions. For the first time I am not covered under my dad's insurance. I need to get busy again, making money, and making things count. The next five years are going to be critical for me and my career. This is my focus. I am always going to play music. I am going to continue to work this brand. That said. I'm going to do what I can to make things happen."

With the turmoil brought on by this pandemic, have you given any serious thought to pursuing songwriting instead of focusing on the performing?

"I have. It has put things in perspective for me. You think that there would never be a time that people could not go to places to hear live music or live events. The pandemic has changed. Here it is in front of us. Everything has stopped. If I had to depend on streaming as my only source of income musically, there is no way I could survive."

Just curious...you, as have others, have been shut down from a performance perspective. All venues, events, even bars have been shut down leaving few if any options available. Songwriting is not dependent on these terms. If your songs are being sold, recorded by other artists is would produce revenue, wouldn't it?

> "Good question. I might add though, even the professionals are not out playing tours. Yeah, the songwriting and radio play might be great, but radio makes their money off advertising and few are spending money on advertising right now. I have talked with a few of the local radio stations. They are suffering as well. They are not getting the advertising dollars. I have asked myself what will be around in times like these. Family will always be around. Beyond them, everything is up in the air. Times are crazy."

Where do you see yourself when the country begins opening back up? In South Carolina nothing related to the entertainment industry has been cleared to open by the governor. At Myrtle Beach where we live, this includes movie theaters, bowling alleys, sports venues, places like the Carolina Opry and Alabama Theater.

> "I will be performing in Myrtle Beach May 16th at Wahoo's in Murrels Inlet. To say I am ready to play is an understatement. I'm hesitant about promoting it on social media because it might backfire on my end, people wondering why I am considering playing during times of social distancing. The venue has policies and procedures in place to protect the customers and entertainers."

We dined out for the first time in ten weeks May 13th. We drove through Murrels Inlet trying to decide what looked safe to test the water. All the venues looked too crowded for our taste and first time trying it, not much social distancing from what we could see from our car. We opted instead for an Outback that had few vehicles in the parking lot. The staff made us feel at ease. This will be a pick and choose time for us for a while. Weighing the risks will be tricky.

> "I have bills to pay so I guess I have to risk getting back out there when options are available. Wahoo's did warn me

that they would not be able to accommodate a large crowd. Capacity is limited according to state regulations right now. Them telling me that was my hint to not try to over promote it.

It does not matter who you are or your status, we are all going through this. Rich, poor or broke it is treating us all the same. If anything, I believe this has brought everyone together like nothing else probably could. This has been a humbling experience. Because I push so hard it is easy to let pride get the best of me, thinking I am doing this and that, and for the most part doing it on my own. Then, when it all hits the fan, I realize I am not doing all of this. It's that perspective thing. We have to trust and believe in God in times like this."

It's funny, I fall into the trap of projecting myself, being an entertainer, thinking I am a star but in the end I am not. I'm supposed to leave that on the stage. It is easy to lose that perspective, leaving the Clay Page on the stage and balancing the Clay Page personal life. Through this experience I feel I have reconnected with the personal Clay Page.

I do not mean to sound arrogant. It has just made life real and realizing how fortunate I am. Some of the people I have always idolized find themselves in the same boat. We all tend to idolize celebrities but, at the end of the day, they are just humans like us. I am just a regular guy coping like everybody else. God's plan might to be to show us that we need to refocus on Him and not on our lives and personal perks.

Changing gears, this is my first year off Idol and here I find myself unable to promote my brand and refocus my career. Last year I couldn't because of Idol. I see those performing on Idol this year, not living the experience I had because of the virus. The top 20 are competing from home instead of on stage. I think this sucks for them, unable to experience what Idol is supposed to project. I think Idol is not as engaged because of this format. Those performing are

> missing the opportunities we had to reach a larger audience and more publicity."

I put a different spin on it for Clay. I liked it better seeing the contestants at their homes with family and friends supporting them. It made it more personable. I felt we got to know them better, being on their home turf during the performances. Less of a stage performance and more humbling for them. It appeared more genuine. It has taken it back to where you started, shooting videos in your bedroom.

> "I have seen mere clips of this year's Idol on social media. I'm just not a TV person. What stinks for them, being on American Idol and now not having anywhere to take it, to utilize the experience with everything basically shut down. Hate to say it, but it is almost like wasted publicity. It is tough for anyone to suggest booking them anywhere with the uncertainty.
>
> For me, I have been trying to focus on the good. I have spent much time researching, watching YouTube videos, and educating myself. Some people have posted songs about how to cut grass and having pretty lawns."

I have noticed a lot of performers writing and singing songs about the pandemic or their experience with it. Have you considered writing a song about it or your experience?

> "If I am being completely honest, I have wondered why I haven't been able to write a song about it. I haven't even tried to write a song about it. My mind has not been in an inspirational mode. For me to sit down and write a song is kind of like the weather; the weather must be exactly right. I cannot think about writing while in survival mode. I have been blessed. Plenty of folks have reached out and given me gifts. Reconnecting and refocusing have become priorities. I am 26 and not anywhere near done. It is a funky spot right now, but we are all going to get through it if you keep the faith and believe in God.

Clay made it to the beach with friends Barron, Tyler, and Jimmy. They booked a charter out of Murrels Inlet for four hours of morning fishing. Clay was reluctant, knowing how badly he and the sun do not get along given his fair skin. Clay and the boys had a great fishing experience with Murrels Inlet Fishing Charters LLC.

An added side note as it relates to Covid-19: Clay's American Idol friend, Laine Hardy, made this announcement on social media July 21st.

> 'This wasn't what I expected on the first day of summer. My doctor confirmed I have Coronavirus, but my symptoms are mild and I'm home recovering in quarantine. Y'all stay safe and healthy.'

Clay suspects he might have contracted it before it had been identified as the risk it has now become. Goes to show no one is immune or safe from this invisible enemy. Prayers continue for those impacted and for a cure to this dreadful virus. Clay holds firm to his belief in God and things happening for a reason.

From the author, T. Allen Winn

Clay and I began this journey during a chance meeting in Abbeville October 2019. My wife and I were visiting friends in Abbeville and staying for a few days. I was also meeting another friend to discuss a book project about his dad. When I am in town, I usually drop in on my pal Benji Greeson. When possible, I sit in on a segment of his radio show, The Southern Fried Morning Show on WZLA 92.9 FM. On this Friday, Benji had scheduled a music guest for the show, so I dropped by afterwards. They were just wrapping up when I arrived.

Benji introduced me to the smiling Clay Page. We exchanged pleasantries. I shared with him that Benji and I had co-written a couple of books about Abbeville Panther's football. I jokingly mentioned to Clay that if he ever desired to tell his story that I might be able to help him with it, that I had my own publishing company, Buttermilk Books. Clay said that would be great. We exchanged information and then he was on his way.

Afterwards, I asked Benji, what was the young man's story? He enlightened me, telling me he was from Elberton and somewhat of a local favorite with an impressing following. He added that he had just participated in the 2019 American Idol and had done quite well, making it to the top 40 and the Hawaii round. It then registered with me that I remembered seeing him on Idol. That was that, not much more to it. A few hours later I was at a local restaurant for lunch when I noticed Clay at the checkout. He and I again exchanged pleasantries before he departed.

Two weeks later young Clay Page contacted me at my home in Myrtle Beach saying he had thought about it and was ready to do a book on his life. Wow. I had just begun another biography for that friend I mentioned. Well, it is not uncommon for me to juggle multiple book projects simultaneously. Mostly, those are my fictional tales. I had never taken on one biography previously and now was faced with doing two. Undaunted, I laid out the plan for doing the book project. A week later we began.

Clay phoned me as he was leaving Elberton and heading to Charlotte, figuring this would be a good time to chat. That chat lasted the entire drive to his destination in Charlotte, nearly three hours. The opening for the book had been recorded. The premise would be Clay reflecting as he made that trip. Talk about opening up, Clay did just that, often surprising himself. For someone I had only met briefly, now I had heard almost everything I was afraid to ask and then some. We developed a comfortable rapport during our first lengthy conversation. This would be the first of many logged hours on the phone.

Not only did I learn a wealth of information about the now 26-year-old singer-songwriter, I think Clay learned even more about himself. He treaded waters long ago forgotten and, yes, he had a few regrets that he reconciled along the way. One being the youngster he had treated terribly in Calhoun Falls. He reached out and apologized, of course. Stepping back and reevaluating oneself can often be somewhat of a cleansing for the soul. Reflection can serve a greater purpose if you allow your mind and heart to absorb and digest what you have learned. Often, I felt like a therapist, listening to his confessions and lessons learned. It was a phone a friend relationship for nearly eight months, having only met him that one encounter in Abbeville. But I knew all I needed to know about him to respect him and know the man beyond the singer persona.

No greater love has there ever been than from those who molded Clay, his mother, Jennifer, and his grandmother, Camilla. I thoroughly enjoyed the conversations with both. Rodney Page, Clay's dad was quite candid during our conversation. I felt like I was visiting with some of my kinfolk when I chatted with Clay's granddaddy James Robinson. Then there are those who impacted his life, mentored, and supported him: Uncle Norman, Papa Ricky, David Jones, and Tubby Worley. Vernon Brown added that smidgen of needed guitar picking internship to round out a young man on a quest. Let's not forget that dirt ditched out by family and friends.

Clay and I logged in countless phone hours as we pieced his life together. I am proud to have been part of this project. Clay Page is as genuine and pure as they come. He credits God and family with him being who he is, and designing the plan set forth so far. Faith and prayer have been a huge part of his life. There is no doubt Clay will face all challenges and he will be successful at whatever he chooses to do with his life. For now, this is music, and this has been his story thus far.

Update: As a result of this book, in mid-June Clay wrote a new song titled 'Working on Myself'.

About the Author

T. Allen Winn, like Clay Page, was born in Abbeville, South Carolina. He began publishing his books in 2011 through Prose Press Publishing. His first seven books were published under this brand. He now publishes his books via his publishing brand, Buttermilk Books. T. Allen and his wife have called the Myrtle Beach area their home since 2005. Follow him on Facebook at T. Allen Winn. His books are sold on Amazon, at Southern Succotash in Abbeville, S.C. and at Grapefull Sisters Vineyard in Tabor City, N.C.

Fiction from T. Allen Winn
The Detective Trudy Wagner series

Road Rage
North of the Border
Tithes and Offerings

Bigfoot Series

Foot, Tree Knockers and Rock Throwers
Another Foot, What Really Happened to D.B. Cooper

More Fiction from T. Allen Winn

The Perfect Spook House
Dark Thirty
Lou Who
Raw Ride, a Wild West Zombie Apocalyptic Shoot'um Up
The Man Who Met the Mouse
Mister Twix Mystery, a Cat Scene Investigation
The Lord's Last Acres, Birth of the Bugsters
The Tenth Elemental
Come Here Getouttahere, Tyler's Tail Wagging Tale

Non-Fiction from T. Allen Winn

Being Bentley, A Dog Like No Other
It's All About the 'A', Faith, Family, Football and Forever to Thee
with coauthor, Benji Greeson
It's All About the Angels in the Backfield, Dawn of a Dynasty
with coauthor, Benji Greeson
December's Darkest Day, While I Breathe, I Hope
The Hardwood Walker of Port Harrelson Road (based on true events in Bucksport, S.C.)
Cuz, My Brother, Life is Good, God is Good
The Endless Mulligan, Short Shots from the Golf Whomper
Clay Page, Somewhere In Between

Memoirs

The Caregiver's Son, Outside the Window Looking In
Cornbread and Buttermilk, Good Ole Fashion
Home Cooked Nostalgic Nonsense
Don't Sit Naked in A Grits Tree, More Nostalgic Nonsense

Short Stories

For Your Amusement featured in
Beach Author Network's book titled 'Shorts'

Ciled Me a Bar featured in friend and author, Danny Kuhn's
Headline Book's *Mountain Mysts*, Honorable Mention in Fiction
at the 2015 London Book Festival and the book
is endorsed by *Joyce Dewitt* of the sitcom *Three's Company*

Short story about his Granny Bowie in friend and author Robert
Sharpe's book, *The Heart and Soul of Caring*,
about caregivers and their challenges

www.ingramcontent.com/pod-product-compliance
Lightning Source LLC
Chambersburg PA
CBHW050105170426
43198CB00014B/2472